CHINAFY

Why China is Leading the West in Innovation and How the Rest of the World Can Catch Up

JOANNA HUTCHINS

Marshall Cavendish
Business

Published in 2023 by Marshall Cavendish Business
An imprint of Marshall Cavendish International

Other Marshall Cavendish Offices:
Marshall Cavendish Corporation, 800 Westchester Ave, Suite N-641, Rye Brook,
NY 10573, USA • Marshall Cavendish International (Thailand) Co Ltd, 253
Asoke, 16th Floor, Sukhumvit 21 Road, Klongtoey Nua, Wattana, Bangkok 10110,
Thailand • Marshall Cavendish (Malaysia) Sdn Bhd, Times Subang, Lot 46,
Subang Hi-Tech Industrial Park, Batu Tiga, 40000 Shah Alam, Selangor Darul
Ehsan, Malaysia

Marshall Cavendish is a registered trademark of Times Publishing Limited

ISBN 978-981-5044-50-8

Printed in Singapore

Contents

Chapter 1 Is It Time to Start Copying China?   7

- The Future Is Already Here, It Is Just Very
  Unevenly Distributed   7
- Innovation Is an Arms Race   11
- It's Time to Copy China   15
- Nine Catalysts to Chinafy Business   16

**Chapter 2 How Did China Emerge as a Global
Innovation Leader? A Brief History**   19

- Workshop to the World   23
- Made in China... for China   27
- The New Landscape of Business   30
- Behind the China Curtain   34

THE CHINAFY CATALYSTS

Chapter 3 Solve the Innovator's Dilemma   37

- Ambidextrous Innovation at the World's Most
  Valuable Unicorn   44
- "Explore" Innovation at ByteDance   46
- ByteDance Delivers Exploit Innovation with
  Growth Hacking   58
- Ambidextrous Operations at ByteDance   58
- How to Export This Catalyst   60

Chapter 4 Become a Bridge Builder   69
- Alibaba Builds a Bridge for E-commerce   72
- Social Commerce   78
- How to Export This Catalyst   81

Chapter 5 Think Like a Futurist   87
- The Future of Drones   91
- The Future of Tea   96
- The Future of Social Influencers   101
- How to Export This Catalyst   104

Chapter 6 Architect New Value Constellations   111
- WeChat: Arguably the Most Powerful Value Constellation in the World   117
- Hema and New Retail Create a Powerful New Value Constellation for Grocery   125
- How to Export This Catalyst   132

Chapter 7 Embrace Small "s" Strategy   137
- Creating the World's Largest Appliance Company   141
- Cool, Not Cold: Small "s" Strategy in Action   145
- How to Export This Catalyst   149

Chapter 8 Drive Reverse Innovation   155
- Medicine for the Masses   159
- Smartphones and Smart Living Democratized   161
- Chinese EVs Poised for Global Domination   165
- Agriculture Joins the Digital Revolution   169
- How to Export This Catalyst   172

Chapter 9 Datafy to Accelerate Business 177
- Tech Startup or Beverage Company? 181
- Data-Hungry "New Retail" Makes Fast Food Smart 183
- Data-Driven Technology Enables Delivery in Minutes 187
- With Data as Strategy, Fast Fashion Becomes Real-Time Retailing 189
- How to Export This Catalyst 193

Chapter 10 Collapse Time 201
- Leaving Competitors in the Dust 205
- Sprinting to Success 207
- Nio Challenges the Automotive Industry 209
- How to Export This Catalyst 213

Chapter 11 Harness Fusion, Unleash New Potential 219
- Yatsen: The Beauty Tech Game-Changer 223
- How to Export This Catalyst 233

A LOOK AHEAD

Chapter 12 The Future for China Growth and the Chinafy Catalysts 239
- China Aims for Global Innovation Domination 244
- In China, Change Is the Only Constant 247
- Why We Must Still Watch and Learn from China 252

Chapter 1

Is It Time to Start Copying China?

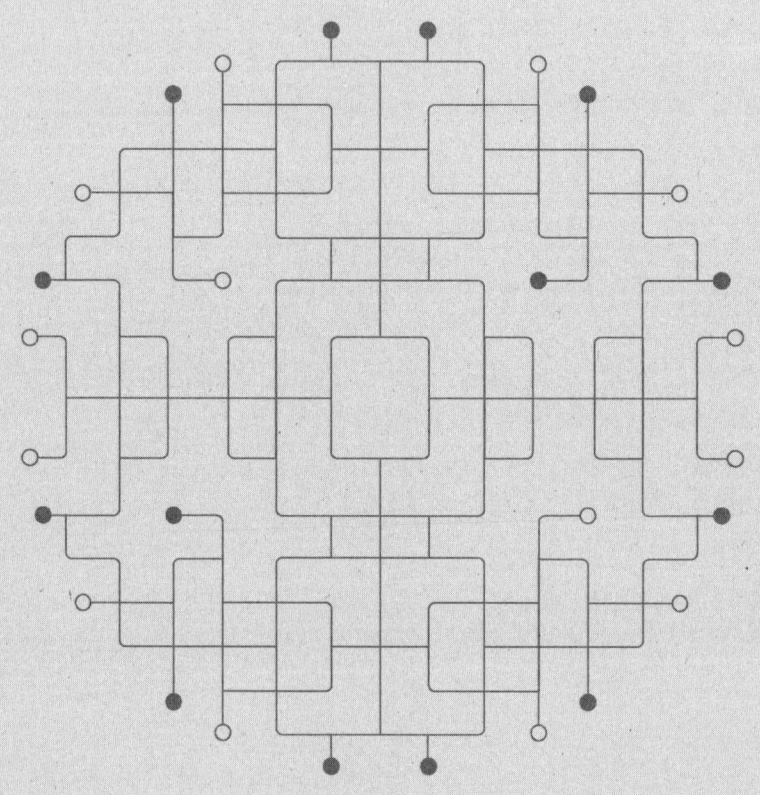

WESTERN BUSINESS LEADERS make two key assumptions about China – that China's success relies on copying the West, and that the West is the seat of true innovation. The truth is surprising. China is both copying *and* innovating, and while Western businesses are busy looking for the next new thing, China is rapidly iterating on what has already been done and pushing ahead. The truth is condemning. We are getting disrupted and left behind, but savvy Western business leaders can learn, innovate, and excel by copying China's playbook.

The Future Is Already Here, It Is Just Very Unevenly Distributed

In William Gibson's 1984 science fiction book *Neuromancer*, a down-on-his-luck cyberhacker hired for one last job faces off with an intelligent computer. Gibson, who popularized the term "cyberspace", is well known for predicting technologies and innovations in his books that are somehow just around the corner. When asked by *The Economist* in 2003 how he predicted artificial intelligence in 1984 when computers were not even yet widely prevalent, Gibson quipped, "The future is already here, it is just very unevenly distributed."

Gibson's sentiment is that invention, innovation and progress are happening all around us, they are just not always visible from where we might personally sit. Further, if we dig into these pockets, we can crystal-ball-gaze and somewhat reliably predict the future. Imagine... somewhere in the world, there are pockets of innovation we do not see with people designing futures filled with technologies and experiences we cannot imagine – be it in a lab in Mumbai, a conference room in Silicon Valley, an office in London or even in someone's garage in a random, nondescript small US town. In principle, the ideas and innovations with potential take hold, and like seeds are propagated and grow. If they are significant and game-changing enough, these seeds spread widely and have global reach and impact. Then later, for those who might not have a bird's-eye view of their isolated beginnings, these innovations seemingly rise from nowhere.

Today, the world has a great many hubs of innovation. There are countries that are nearly cashless, countries where electric taxis and public transport are the norm, where public health and safety are managed centrally with big data and artificial intelligence, and autonomous vehicles make not just same-day, but within-the-hour, home deliveries. This isn't science fiction. This is not even across multiple countries. This is China. China has emerged as one of the most advanced and technology-driven markets in the world with a largely cashless society driven by world-leading digital ecosystems. The future is here, and it is in China.

Unfortunately, in recent years from 2020 to 2023, this is happening behind the closed borders of a global pandemic. With little access to China, due to extremely limited entry permits and extended, mandatory government quarantines, business leaders globally have been unable to, or have chosen not to, visit and as a result are losing sight of the unprecedented progress that is underway. Some say China was already 10 years ahead of the rest of the world with its digital ecosystems, cashless economy, frictionless lifestyle in society, and significant advancements in artificial intelligence and big data. And the technology approach used by China to manage Covid-19 has only accelerated this already fast-moving, innovative society. But sadly, the Great Firewall of China works both ways, limiting information not only into, but also out of the country. Further, many of the technology platforms are unique to China, so are not visible to anyone outside the country. The only great exception to this being Douyin/TikTok – which has permeated globally and taken the social media world by storm. So, while China is advancing in innovation, for the most part it is happening without visibility to the rest of the world. And for businesses that compete globally to remain competitive in the face of a rising China, this insight is highly pertinent, if not essential.

Innovation Is an Arms Race

Innovation is imperative for societies to grow and thrive, evolving and progressing towards more promising futures. Today, we are all racing towards brighter futures globally. Innovation is in fact the new arms race. Those societies that push ahead in innovation will be the global thought leaders and superpowers of the world. However, the Western-dominant past when it comes to societies and innovation does create some biases on how the West views China and innovation.

Western business leaders have an avid curiosity about China, seeing it as both an opportunity and a threat. Interest in China has grown in the Western world, as China represents a vast potential market for Western businesses. In 2019, the World Bank Group reported that China's GDP was increasing at a rate of 10% annually, lifting its predominantly impoverished population to the middle class. China's population now represents nearly 19% of the world's population. Leveraging China's business-friendly regulations and low labour costs, Western businesses have been moving manufacturing and operations to China since the 1970s.

However, this increased exposure and exploitative interest in China has only served to bolster our beliefs in the West's dominance. Ironically, we've become blind to what is really happening and the ways in which Chinese innovation is propelling its own society into the future, actually surpassing Western civilizations. *Chinafy* challenges several underlying assumptions and perspectives that Western business leaders hold regarding Chinese business practices and serves as a bold invitation to open their eyes and reclaim their innovative roots.

In fact, Western businesses, especially in the United States, have a long legacy of innovation – from steel titan Andrew Carnegie and oil tycoon John D. Rockefeller to modern-day moguls like Steve Jobs and Bill Gates. The inventions and innovations of the Industrial Revolution enabled the Western world to scale new businesses exponentially, providing the foundation for the success and wealth the Western world enjoys today and creating a confidence that the West will always dominate. The problem, however, is that we've become too complacent, too entrenched in the old ways of invention, and we've forgotten what innovation is really about. Like the hare in Aesop's fable, we're napping on the sidelines, overly confident in our prowess. While we sleep, China is pushing ahead, innovating around invention, and scaling technology adoptions at a rapid pace. We're getting left behind.

Let us look at digital cashless payments as a case in point. Digital cashless payment technologies emerged nearly simultaneously in the US and China in the early 2000s. Two decades on, China is

551 times greater in total expenditures on mobile payment versus the US, the world's leading economy. Specifically, in 2019, digital payment adoption in China was greater than 80% of the population, with approximately $54 trillion in spending on mobile payments. Since 2019, in many outlets in China, payment can be made by letting cameras scan your face – there is no need to even liberate your smartphone from your pocket. Compare this to the US trajectory of digital payments, which totalled only US$98bn in 2019.

Some say China copied this technology, that they did not invent it. In fact, oddly enough, the first digital wallet was by The Coca Cola Company in the US in 1997, not Apple or even a bank. But if we focus on the invention, we are missing the point. All inventions or technologies are ultimately "copied", typically in 10 years when a patent expires. The real question is, how did China explode digital payment systems to completely transform society in a way that the US did not – especially considering that Alipay and Apple Pay launched in the same year, 2014? What can we learn from that about how to accelerate innovation adoption beyond the middle class in big cities, to even rural users without bank accounts and seemingly no need for portability of payment? And why, nearly 20 years on with digital payments technology – in an ostensibly more developed culture and economy, sometimes described as cutting-edge, with greater access to the internet, technology and infrastructure – is the US still so slowly climbing the digital payments adoption curve? To bring this into sharper relief, as of May 2021, Apple reports that 24% of iPhone users use Apple Pay. As of July 2022, 45.4m Americans used Apple Pay to make at least one transaction in the last month.[1] Whereas in China in 2022, 90% of the entire population

---

1.   Money Transfers Report on Apple Pay, "15 Amazing Apple Pay Statistics for

of 1.426bn uses digital payment services, regardless of Android or Apple platform.[2]

In considering this, let us pause for a moment to distinguish between invention and innovation. Invention is the creation of a product or process for the first time, e.g., Xerox Parc's initial creation of the operating system and optical mouse technology. Whereas innovation builds, improves upon or connects existing ideas to create a new-to-market product, process or service for which customers will pay – thus commercializing opportunities and often catapulting them into the mainstream, e.g., Steve Jobs's application of the aforementioned Xerox Parc technology in Apple personal computers to transform the user experience.[3]

So while it is undeniable that China's reputation is beleaguered by accusations and even evidence of intellectual property theft, there is no doubt that China is innovating. Given the same tools and technologies as others, they make more of them – make them bigger, faster and more impactful in society and commercially. We have to hold in our hands this paradox, that both can be true: China can both be riding on the tail of others' inventions *and* innovating at the same time.

Another common refrain is that China's progress is routinely attributed to government policies such as industry protectionism,

---

2022 That Will Surprise You", moneytransfers.com, September 26, 2022. https://moneytransfers.com/news/content/apple-pay-statistics#:~:text=Apple%20Pay%20is%20supported%20by,transaction%20in%20the%20last%20month.

2.   HBR IdeaCast, Episode 791, Interview with Zak Dychtwald, "How Tech Adoption Fuels China's Innovation Boom", May 4, 2021. https://hbr.org/podcast/2021/05/how-tech-adoption-fuels-chinas-innovation-boom

3.   Teppo Felin and Todd Zenger, "What sets breakthrough strategies apart", *MIT Sloan Management Review*, 59, Vol.59(2), 2017.

restrictive operating requirements for foreign companies that inhibit competitiveness, non-replicable market conditions such as its sheer size and scale. It is this narrative than often discounts China's innovation and even looks at it derisively, without exploring its very real success in commercializing technology and innovation for exponential growth.

The risk of these counter-narratives is that the real seeds of innovation do not propagate globally. If we let the China innovation story be discounted, explained away and written off, the rest of the world will be left behind as China inches ahead in the societal arms race of innovation.

It's Time to Copy China

International business leaders often watch China's progress with a mixture of curiosity and distrust, and our politics reinforce this perspective of Chinese innovation as a threat to Western business. Granted, there is undeniable evidence of China's "copycat" business practices – and yet, there's equal evidence of China's ingenuity in scaling and capitalizing on Western invention. We have to make room in our perspective for both truths. What if we stripped away the judgments, ignored the politics, and took a page out of China's playbook to learn from their real stories of success? In other words, what if *we* copied *China*? Not necessarily to beat them, but to, at very least, join them in the next great innovation revolution.

History shows us that great societies, empires, and even world-leading investment banks in recent history, are never too big to fail. It is often a dangerous combination of arrogance and ignorance that precipitates these collapses: arrogance as the dominant culture that their own culture and society are superior, and a wilful ignorance of their own shortcomings, and that others are innovating and will soon eclipse them.

If China happens to be innovating more rapidly and with more social and commercial impact than the rest of the world, where will the rest of the world be in 20 years by comparison? What about even in a mere 10 years? With this in mind, just what are the biggest drivers of China's innovation, and what can the rest of the world learn from China? Are there repeatable models? In fact, there are.

Nine Catalysts to Chinafy Business

Chinafy guides Western business leaders in understanding and applying key principles for innovation that Chinese businesses have been quietly and successfully implementing for years. To achieve this transformation, we must redefine innovation itself. Western business leaders often see innovation as creating something entirely new out of nothing; but Chinese business leaders see innovation as incremental shifts toward exploiting and commercializing an idea. We've mistaken invention for innovation. It's not just about creating new products to sell in the same old ways and through the same systems; it's about looking holistically at every piece of the supply chain and route to market and finding new ways to iterate on the system itself. Innovation builds, improves upon, or connects existing ideas to commercialize and scale adoption into the mainstream.

Chinafy will help Western business leaders transform their practices and rapidly scale growth through compelling case studies. Readers will learn how to:

- Let go of big "S" Strategy and adopt small "s" strategies to increase operational agility.

- Stop creating and iterating new product developments linearly and create new value constellations in the form of networks and linkages to unleash commercial impact.
- Innovate around inventions to accelerate adoption, instead of relying on existing systems.
- Use data to transform the customer experience and disrupt business-as-usual.
- Spend less time planning and more time sprinting in order to capture market potential and make competition irrelevant.

Specifically, nine key lessons have been distilled from innovation in China to unlock business potential anywhere in the world. In effect, these lessons serve as catalysts for "Chinafying" innovation for growth. These learnings are from the unique ways Chinese companies approach problem-solving, and emerge from very real case-studies of success in China. What is particularly surprising about these insights and lessons is that they demonstrate that the power of transformation and value creation may be closer at hand and less complex than we previously imagined. Innovation does not have to be a hard slog with an unwieldy, massive organizational transformation agenda. It can sometimes even be easy with a small shift in perspective.

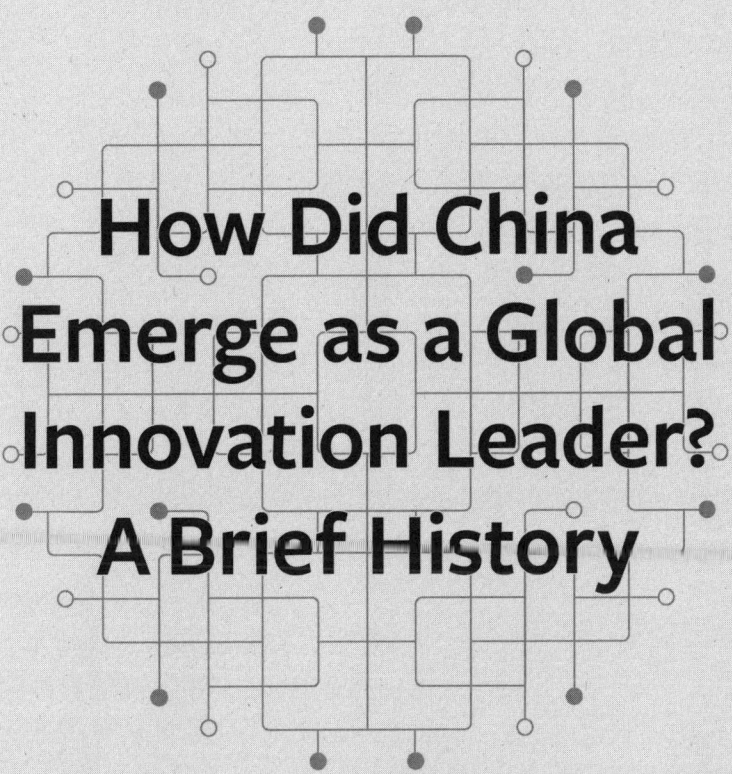

Chapter 2

How Did China Emerge as a Global Innovation Leader? A Brief History

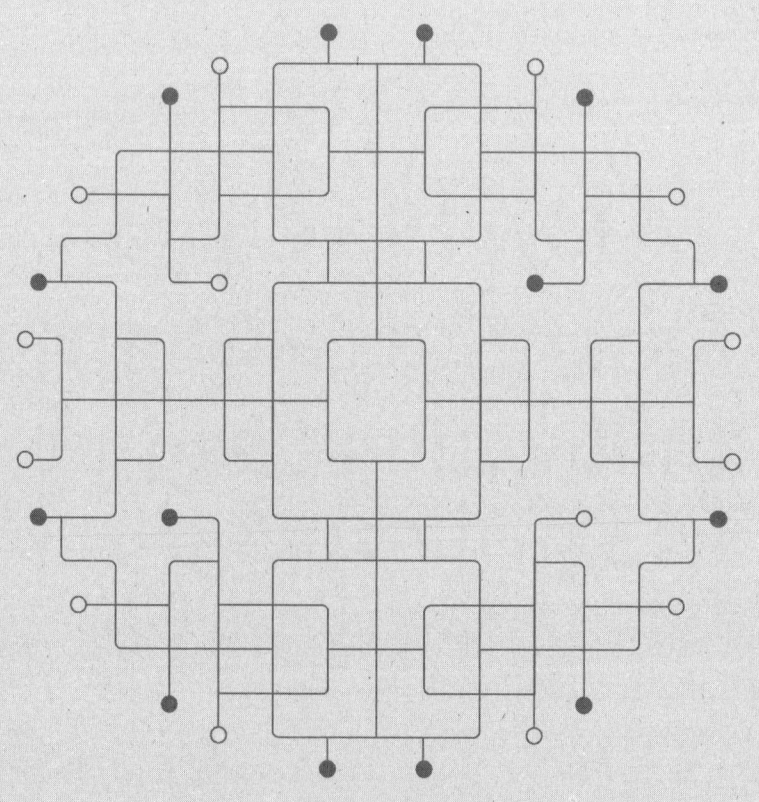

ONE OF THE historical consequences of Mao Zedong's chaotic and violent Cultural Revolution from 1966 to 1976 is that it is currently in the world's collective memory as possibly the most memorable part of Chinese history. What this overshadows is what is most vital for understanding innovation in China today: the great legacy of Chinese discovery, invention, and innovation over the entire course of human history.

Possibly the most famous and well-known inventions from China are the compass, paper-making, printing and gunpowder. Known as the "Four Great Inventions", named as such by the English philosopher Francis Bacon, given the impact they had upon the world. All four inventions made their way to Europe by way of Arab traders bringing them from their travels in China. The compass is traced back to China's Warring States period (475 BC–221 BC) and is credited with spawning the Age of Exploration, the era of great European sea exploration and colonization in the 15th century. Printing is traced to before the 8th century and usually attributed to Emperor Wen of Sui, who ordered the recording of Buddhist scriptures. Gunpowder was invented for use in fireworks for major festivals in the 9th century and by the 12th century had been perfected and calibrated for use in weaponry in the form of bullets, cannonballs and land mines.

Beyond the big four, we see China having some of the most advanced metallurgy, hydraulics, engineering, architecture, agriculture, and mathematics recorded around the time of the Shang dynasty (1600 BC–1050 BC). The use of a plough in the Neolithic period from circa 3000 BC to 2000 BC enabled high agricultural yields, making China one of the wealthiest and most abundant places in the world at that time. By the 1st century, Chinese sailors developed the rudder for steering at sea, sailing as far as East Africa, and in the Song dynasty (960–1279 AD) paper money was invented to facilitate more complex exchanges and international trading as a result of their sea travels.

These are things in the West we have forgotten, or frankly perhaps never knew, as history classes in the West do not often explore Asia with any great depth until World War II. Further, in the realm of modern-day politics, the rest of the world is often focused on the negatives and allow these to overshadow the positives of the progress being made in China. A scan of the international news and its presentation of China is more likely to yield topics like intellectual property protections, environmental concerns, trade wars and humanitarian issues surrounding child labour and ethnic minority groups. And while those topics are certainly deserving of the world's attention, it should also be understood that stories of Chinese innovation are well and alive in China and form the basis of the Chinese psyche, with most individuals holding this innovative and pioneering history as a form of deeply ingrained values and beliefs about what their society was and still is today. We need to understand that much like post-World War II America, in the Chinese culture there is a great optimism and belief in China's ability to invent, innovate, and transform the world. And the shared belief of 1.4bn people is a very powerful force.

To understand the China of now and the future, we need to both remember the centuries of past that inform the Chinese cultural legacy as well as recognize how recent social and economic developments further instil and reinforce beliefs and culture of China as an innovative society among Chinese nationals. To illuminate the more recent Chinese culture of innovation, we will take a brief look at how the last 50 years have shaped China's course of development and elevated the country into a major and highly influential force in the world.

Workshop to the World

The 1970s saw rising demand for consumer electronics and consumer products in the West. When China entered the World Trade Organization (WTO) in 2010 the rules were established for international trade and investment, making China a plausible option for global businesses to enter and expand into. At the time, China's uneducated workforce, lax labour laws, and US-friendly tax environment made it the ideal location for outsourcing the manufacturing of these highly demanded goods. In fact, "70% of China's economic achievements this decade [from 2010 to 2020] can be attributed to our membership in the WTO," says Zhang Hanlin, head of the China Institute for WTO Studies at the University of International Business and Economics in Beijing.[4]

China's cheap, uneducated labour force was incredibly attractive to countries and industries for whom labour costs were becoming prohibitive. As a result, today, whole industries have disappeared from some countries in the EU and the US and have landed squarely in China's lap. For example, 70% of the shoes sold in the US are

---

4.   Peter Ford, "How WTO Membership Made China the Workshop of the World", *Christian Science Monitor*, December 14, 2011. https://www.csmonitor.com/World/Asia-Pacific/2011/1214/How-WTO-membership-made-China-the-workshop-of-the-world

imported from China, with the industry employing 288m Chinese migrant workers in the southern Chinese city of Dongguan.[5] China now dominates the global industry of shoe manufacturing, and as a result, a large population of Chinese are better off as the shoe workers earn 5–10x more than is possible in the mostly agricultural opportunities in their home towns. Thanks to this win-win situation – the world's need for cheap labour and the better and higher paying jobs it brought to China – during this 10-year stretch, trade increased 5x for China, making it the world's biggest exporter.[6]

China's trade boom helped other nations as well. While manufacturing jobs were lost in other countries, this had the effect of forcing the workforces of these countries to upskill and move into careers with more value-add to the overall economies. In November 2011, deputy Commerce Minister Yu Jianhua said Chinese imports "have become a major driving force for global economic growth", and estimated that 14m jobs have been created abroad as a result.[7]

Overall, manufacturing and trade with China was of global benefit – keeping prices down for everyday goods and thus keeping inflation low in US and EU, enabling their economies to move upstream in capabilities while also providing better job opportunities for China's largely rural workforce at the time. However, there were accusations and evidence of intellectual property (IP) and piracy violations. As China sought to develop businesses on par with the US and EU, heavy "borrowing" of IP became a common method as it adopted technologies and methods from the companies that

5.   Jennifer Pak, "The Chinese Workers Who Make Your Shoes", market-place.org, October 2, 2019. https://www.marketplace.org/2019/10/02/the-chinese-workers-who-make-your-shoes/
6.   Ford, "How WTO Membership Made China the Workshop of the World".
7.   Ford, "How WTO Membership Made China the Workshop of the World".

outsourced to them. Piracy was an issue in particular for software and entertainment products. For example, Microsoft revealed in 2011 that although the same number of PCs were sold in the US and China, the Microsoft OS and software licences sold in China were only about 5% of its US revenues.[8]

Amidst the unresolved challenges and controversies around IP as well as views that progress was potentially usurped, the Chinese economy thrived, growing faster than any nation in the world. And the skeptics within China who said that by entering international trade, China was leaving itself vulnerable to attack by "dancing with wolves",[9] started to assert that China had in fact triumphed over the West, leveraging foreign capital and investment to propel China into the modern age. The manufacturing-fuelled economic boom did indeed pull China's largely rural population out of hunger and poverty and created a growing middle class. China's government further leaned into this momentum and began to drive social and economic development with various domestic policies and long-term plans. Education was prioritized to further advance the society, with a focus on science and mathematics to educate a highly skilled workforce. The lack of infrastructure – roads, airports, trains, public transport and even development of residential homes – was prioritized as another key area to address and provided opportunities for entrepreneurial ventures, giving rise to new technologies and fast-growing businesses.

In the subsequent years, thanks to the jobs and the rise of China's middle class, the West started to see China as both a workplace of the world as well as a market for the world's goods. More than just

---

8.   Ford, "How WTO Membership Made China the Workshop of the World".
9.   Ford, "How WTO Membership Made China the Workshop of the World".

manufacturing, international companies opened corporate offices and operations in China, marketing their international brands and products to Chinese consumers – and quite successfully. Due to various quality scandals, including the infamous case of melamine in infant milk formula in 2008, many Chinese consumers preferred international brands. There was a common belief that international companies and brands had higher standards of quality and processes for quality checks as well as greater investments into R&D – all areas that consumers suspected Chinese companies might be weak in. International brands and marketing investment further accelerated the consumer boom and led to further upskilling of the Chinese labour force as they moved into corporate jobs in marketing, sales, R&D, legal and finance for international companies.

Of course, rapid modernization and industrialization had its downsides. Quality issues were real and forced greater regulatory control to protect consumers. With increased manufacturing to meet both local and overseas demand for goods, China's resulting environmental pollution challenges became a serious public health issue for China and the world. Further, relentless industrialization spurred migration to urban centres, resulting in densely packed cities with high-intensity work cultures and for some, low quality of life. Cases of death from overwork were reported in the media and intensely discussed on social media by Chinese netizens.

Around this time, with China's "bad news" being pervasive in international media and witnessing how social media had helped to enable the Arab Spring overseas, the Chinese government reacted strongly, enacting what is known as "The Great Firewall" in 2009, banning access to all international media, search engines, email systems, social media, and news sources. Further, China was starting to see the influence of trade globalization also having the impact of globalization of thought and moved to actively curtail Western influences and thinking. Foreign textbooks were banned in schools as well as the teaching of "Western Thought". Efforts to censor unfavourable reports domestically were also dramatically increased – with no freedom of speech, the Cyberspace Administration of China (CAC) reviewed, filtered, and deleted any unfavourable content and further had the authority to arrest and indefinitely detain the individuals responsible for generating the content. These concerns and desire to reduce exposure to Western thinking gave rise to a new phase in China's development: a nation turning inward, focused on developing its own home-grown domestic businesses and industries.

Made in China... for China

As China came into its own as a growing economy and burgeoning epicentre of business, it instituted a 10-year national strategic plan and industrial policy, "Made in China 2025". With a focus on high-tech sectors, China sought to move upstream in the value chain of industry, moving away from labour-intensive industries and reducing its reliance on Western technologies, to become a technology-intensive global powerhouse in its own right. The Made in China 2025 programme aimed to use government subsidies and tax breaks, mobilize SOEs, and advance IP development and acquisition to catch up with, and eventually surpass, the West. The focus of the programme was around what is known as the Fourth Industrial Revolution – the fusion of advances in AI, robotics, the Internet of Things (IoT), genetic engineering, big data and quantum computing. Key industries with high potential growth became areas of strategic investment, including IT, telecommunications, new energy vehicles and transport, advanced robotics particularly in manufacturing and biotech, agricultural and maritime technologies, aerospace engineering and AI.

An initial step in the Made in China 2025 plan was to move manufacturing upstream. Original Equipment Manufacturers (OEMs) were actively encouraged to leverage their manufacturing knowledge to create domestic brands. Subsidies and tax breaks provided incentives to do so and suddenly a flood of domestic brands were made in China – for Chinese consumers. These brands and businesses were offering the same high-quality products sold overseas but adapted for the Chinese market. For example, dishwashers and washing machines were smaller to fit into smaller homes and had fewer bells and whistles but maintained the features relevant to the local market. Sporting goods brands emerged that offered high-quality running shoes and sporting gear but at extremely affordable prices, making athletics and street style accessible to young Chinese consumers. Essentially Chinese consumers of lower to middle incomes could now afford modern conveniences and even luxuries typically only available to the upper middle class or wealthy.

Additionally, the Chinese government funnelled even more energy and investment into the education system, with a clear focus on STEM education. Today, there are more PhD STEM graduates in China each year than in the US, and the gap is further widening. A report released by Georgetown University's Center for Security and Emerging Technology in 2021 projects that by 2025, China's annual STEM PhD graduates will be double those in the US.[10]

10.   Michael T. Nietzel, "U.S. Universities Fall Further Behind China in Production of STEM PhDs", *Forbes*, August 7, 2021. https://www.forbes.com/sites/michaeltnietzel/2021/08/07/us-universities-fall-behind-china-in-production-of-stem-phds/

The Chinese tech boom was accelerated as result of this national focus. The internet economy emerged as Alibaba Group pioneered e-commerce, and other domestic companies such as JD.com launched competing platforms. Some of the biggest names in tech in China emerged during this phase. Huawei, now present in over 170 countries, became a global player in telecommunications, mobile phones, electronics and smart devices with high-performing technology at attractive prices – surpassing Apple in smartphones sold globally in 2018[11] and winning bids globally for large government contracts. Chinese computer and server maker Lenovo acquired IBM's PC business and became a global PC powerhouse. BYD quietly took over the global electric bus market, with nearly 80% of the world's electric buses used for public transport being from this previously unheard-of Chinese battery and electric vehicle manufacturer.[12] China-based DJI became the world's leading drone manufacturer. Tencent emerged as a world-leading gaming company and started WeChat. The list goes on and on.

With the staggering amount of innovation and value creation by Chinese businesses during this period, "Made in China" became a mark of pride for a new generation of Chinese entrepreneurs. Many previously successful international brands and businesses began to suffer. Employees no longer sought to work at big multinationals as they seemed old-fashioned and slow-moving compared to local companies, and international brands began to fall out of favour with

---

11. Samuel Gibbs, "Huawei beats Apple to become second-largest smartphone maker", *The Guardian*, August 1, 2018.

12. Research and Markets Report, "Global Electric Bus Market (Value, Volume) – Analysis By Propulsion Type (Battery, Hybrid, Fuel Cell), Consumer, By Region, By Country (2022 Edition): COVID-19 Implications, Competition, and Forecast (2022–2027)", April 25, 2022.

the new Chinese middle class who started to gravitate to domestic brands as a demonstration of national pride. The rise of *guochao* – a desire to buy Chinese goods and services to connect with local roots – has emerged as a driving force in the economy. Baidu searches (the Google search of China) for Chinese brands increased from 38% to 70% of all brand searches from 2009 to 2019, with millennials leading the way in domestic purchasing.[13]

The New Landscape of Business

China was once, centuries ago, the world's biggest economy. It is the government's ambition that China recapture this distinction – and many global analysts expect this will be the case. Indeed, China's progress over the last 30 years towards the goal of becoming an economic superpower is staggering. Today, China has 145 companies on Fortune's Global 500 list – up from just three companies in 1994, surpassing the US, who now only has 124.[14] In 2016, China's GDP overtook the US in terms of purchasing power parity – a method of GDP measurement that calculates the cost of a standard list of goods and services in each country – meaning it has already become one of the world's largest consumer economies. Personal wealth is increasing dramatically – it was predicted by McKinsey that from 2020 to 2025, the number of Chinese millionaires would

13.   Daniel Zipser, Jeongmin Song, Jonathan Woetzel, "Five Consumer Trends Shaping the Next Decade of Growth in China", McKinsey White Paper, November 11, 2021. https://www.mckinsey.com/cn/our-insights/our-insights/five-consumer-trends-shaping-the-next-decade-of-growth-in-china
14.   Clay Chandler, "Chinese Corporations Now Dominate the Fortune Global 500", *Fortune*, August 19, 2022. https://fortune.com/2022/08/18/fortune-global-500-china-companies-profitable-profitability-us-rivals/

double from 5m to 10m.[15] The wealth and value creation in China in the last five decades is unmatched in human history.

Also as part of the Made in China 2025 policy, China has been on a buying spree, acquiring key companies or dominant stakes in companies in strategic industries. It would seem the goal is not to wrangle market share to gain traction in overseas markets but rather to enable access to key resources or facilitate knowledge transfer to China. In many cases, the Chinese acquirers treat the acquisition as more of a partnership, giving the acquired company greater access to China and leveraging their expertise to increase China's own growth and global competitiveness. A few key examples include:

- Chinese automotive manufacturer Geely acquired Volvo, Saab, and The London Taxi Company to enable car design and manufacturing knowledge transfer for growth in the China automotive market.
- State-owned China Ocean Shipping Co. (COSCO) acquired over a dozen ports, mainly in Europe, across the Netherlands, Greece, Spain, Belgium, Italy, Turkey and France, as well as in North Africa and the Indian subcontinent. The stated strategic intent was greater control and access to shipping and logistics, but some do question if there is military intent.
- China's largest meat processor, Shuanghui International Holdings (now WH Group), bought the world's largest hog producer and processor, Smithfield Farms, making it the biggest Chinese takeover of a US company in history. In the US, pork consumption per capita is declining and trails beef and chicken, but in China, pork is the #1 source of protein.

---

15.   Zipser et al., "Five Consumer Trends".

- The US's 100-year-old GE's home appliances division was sold to China's Haier group, which was China's largest acquisition of an electronics business. As China's middle class grows in wealth, Chinese consumers crave modern household conveniences.
- In the energy sector, China's Yanzhou Coal took over Australia's Felix Resources, while China's Sinopec oil and gas company acquired the Swiss-registered oil and gas company Addax, thus further ensuring China's future supply of energy resources for its increasingly energy-hungry population.
- Chinese-dominated Canyon-Bridge, a Cayman Islands-based firm, bought a majority stake in UK-headquartered Imagination, a leading technology company making smartphone chips. For the world's biggest smartphone market, access to components is critical.
- Xi'an Aircraft Industry Corporation (XAC), a subsidiary of the state-owned Aviation Industry Corporation of China (AVIC), bought more than 90% of Austria's Fischer Advanced Composite Components (FACC), one of the leading suppliers of the composites used in everything from airplane wings to engine nacelles and cabins. This gave China access to a large stable of experienced engineers to leverage in its own aircraft development programmes.
- China National Chemical Corporation (ChemChina) acquired a French manufacturer of animal nutrition additives. Adisseo is the world's second-largest producer of methionine, a key additive used in the poultry industry, with a global market share of 29%. Poultry is the second-largest protein source in the Chinese diet.

Yet another recent trajectory in the China business landscape is more Chinese brands and startups looking outside China for growth – some even selling only overseas and not in China at all. A few examples include:

- SHEIN is a China-based, Chinese-owned fashion and lifestyle e-retailer, delivering a global fast fashion proposition that reaches customers in over 150 countries, with its top markets being the US, EU, and Russia – so successful that it is now larger than Zara globally. SHEIN is not available in the China market.
- Beijing-based ByteDance is the most valuable startup unicorn in the world after only 10 years of operation thanks to the global success of its TikTok social media app.
- China's wildly successful Xiaomi IoT brand now enjoys the position as the best-selling smartphone brand in India.
- Guangdong-based Miniso, a retailer of toys, beauty and household products, is opening retail stores overseas with a goal to become the world leader in $10-and-under stores. Its newly opened flagship store in New York City's trendy SoHo neighbourhood is delivering $1m sales per day at a 50% margin[16] – well above its margins in China, where shoppers expect even lower prices.

---

16.   Evelyn Cheng, "Chinese Companies Look to US and Asia as Growth Slows at Home", CNBC, July 12, 2022. https://www.cnbc.com/2022/07/12/chinese-companies-look-to-us-and-asia-as-growth-slows-at-home.html

Behind the China Curtain

Many international business travellers have not been able to visit China since 2019 due to the zero-Covid policies. If they did, they would be surprised at what they would see. Today, China is a completely cashless society – even the homeless accept and prefer digital payment as few stores take cash anymore. There are more smartphone users in China than anywhere in the world, and at 953m users, this is more than India, US, Brazil and Russia combined.[17] QR codes are common as personal digital identification, and a single code is used to access nearly everything in everyday life, from metro entry and hospital records to signifying health status in Covid times – advanced track-and-trace technology turns codes yellow or red if you have been exposed. AI regulates everything from your social media feed to the traffic flow to your coffee menu. The fastest maglev (magnetic levitation) train in the world takes you from Shanghai International Airport to Longyang Road (a distance of 30 km, or 19 miles) in seven minutes. E-commerce orders are delivered to consumers' doors within minutes by autonomous driving vehicles, and in some supermarkets food can be scanned to show the item's point of origin and the details of its journey from the farm to the shelf. The streets are filled with electric vehicles (EVs), with EV sales growing 7x faster than the entire sales elsewhere in the world combined.[18]

Yet, somehow, we are distracted or possibly misinformed about China. We often still view China as a workshop to the world, or we

---

17.   Statista, "Number of Smartphone Users in Leading Countries 2021", statistia. com, Published August 11, 2022. https://www.statista.com/statistics/748053/ worldwide-top-countries-smartphone-users/

18.   Zipser, et al., "Five Consumer Trends".

focus on a prevailing narrative of China as a copycat country, or we worry about security and privacy issues as Chinese apps and games become popular in Western culture. However, the truth is that innovation is propelling China into the future faster than we can imagine – and there is a great deal we can learn from China. If we're smart enough to pay attention, the China of today can provide a glimpse into our own future.

So, come behind the China curtain and unpack nine catalysts to extrapolate learnings from China that can enable exponential growth. But know that in doing so, you may have to challenge yourself on any assumptions not only about China, but also about innovation. With these lessons, business leaders are poised not just to lead greater growth, but to dramatically accelerate the technological advances that will change and advance the shape of global culture and economies.

Here is how each Chinafy catalyst will be broken down:

- **Chinafy lesson explained:** The core concept or nugget – in essence, what precisely is the repeatable model?
- **Supporting case study, data, interviews and/or real-life insights:** Examples of real businesses and outcomes that allow us to deeply understand and metabolize the lesson. Some cases are brief while others are in-depth, but all examples are intended to help us unpack the catalyst.
- **How to export to the rest of the world:** Why this is bigger than China and how could or should this be applied to unlock growth or opportunity? Also, what are the potential downsides, risks or other considerations in applying the catalyst and learnings?

Unless you follow Chinese business with keen interest or have lived in China, some of these businesses and names will not be familiar. This is incredible in and of itself as many of these businesses are generating enormous value, disrupting technology and economies globally, and stand to be world-dominant enterprises. So, to help better gauge their size, scale and impact, where possible, they are compared with well-known Western corollary businesses. Some of these comparisons will be eye-opening, no doubt driving home the point of why these unheard-of companies and businesses are worth a closer look.

Chapter 3

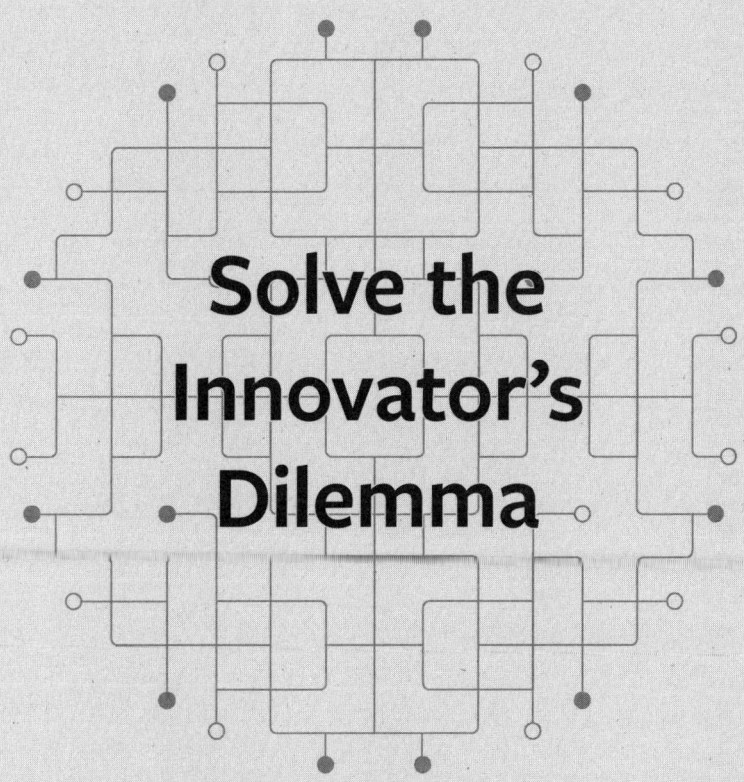

Solve the Innovator's Dilemma

CATALYST 1

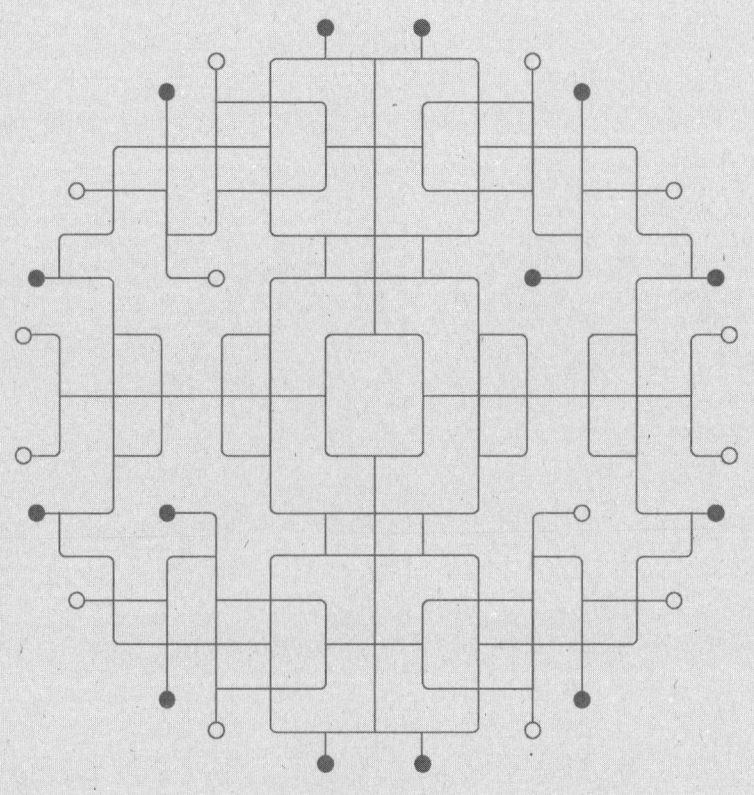

"DISRUPTION" IS A BUZZWORD that has been used for decades. Every business wants to be a "disruptor", and no business wants to be "disrupted". But what does it really mean? Disruption was mentioned more than 10,000 times in articles in the last year[19] – but most people get it wrong. They use the word loosely to invoke the concept of innovation or as a verbal shorthand to describe competition or any situation in which an industry is shaken up. In fact, disruptive innovation theory is more like the story of David and Goliath, when a small and unassuming competitor triumphs over a seemingly undefeatable giant. In the story of David and Goliath, David's weapon is a small stone that he picks up from the ground to topple the giant – an item that does not seem to be a weapon at all and looks unlikely to counter Goliath's armoury of swords and knives. In the case of disruptive innovation, it is almost always the business model that disrupts – we can think of this as the stone – and not a product or service.

The American economist Clayton M. Christensen put forward the fundamental premises of disruptive innovation in his 1997 book, *The Innovator's Dilemma*. Disruptive innovation happens when a smaller company with markedly fewer resources surprisingly, yet successfully, challenges and unseats a large, established incumbent.

---

19. Clayton M. Christensen, Michael E. Raynor, Rory McDonald, "What is Disruptive Innovation?", *Harvard Business Review Magazine*, December 2015.

Disruption by small startups has been a vexing problem for business leaders for decades, not just since the 1990s when the term was popularized.

How does David overturn Goliath, despite his size and power? Well, despite the established, large incumbents having much deeper pockets in addition to greater visibility and access to game-changing industry trends and technologies, they often become myopic – tending to focus on improving existing offers with existing customers, and failing to innovate in new spaces with new customers and to identify and create new realities and futures for their industry.

Christensen calls this conundrum the "innovators' dilemma" – the dilemma being that the success, know-how and profitability of the existing offer often traps incumbents, anchoring them to their current lines of business and rendering them blind to the future of their industries. As a result, breakthrough, disruptive opportunities are stifled or abandoned prematurely from developing in big businesses.

Disruptive innovations by challengers typically employ less-understood emerging technologies, appeal to new and different customers from the incumbents (initially), require different organizational capabilities, and are offered at a lower price point, meaning the opportunity is less profitable and therefore less attractive than the incumbent's core business. And why would a large, successful company margin-down their business and compromise profitability to invest valuable funds and resources in a less attractive enterprise? Shareholders alone would not allow it. But in not doing so, they often miss the opportunities that are essential to their survival. So, completing the metaphor, Goliath's weak point in this case is the combination of performance hurdles, profitability targets, and expert operational capabilities in the current business.

Video streaming services like Netflix disrupting Blockbuster video rentals is one of the classic cases of disruptive innovation, where the established incumbent failed to recognize the emerging potential of the internet as a channel for a lower-cost, convenient service that would better meet consumers' needs. Kodak is yet another example. Despite inventing the world's first digital camera, Kodak failed to recognize that the digital disruption of photography would unseat their mainstay business of film and photo processing.

Christensen's proposed solution to the innovator's dilemma is to spin off innovation to a new business unit, treating it as an incubator operating independently to prospect the future – with more freedom and less hierarchy and bureaucracy versus the core business. In Christensen's terminology, managing innovation is known as an "explore" activity, where new realities can be explored, relieved of rigorous operational and financial constraints. Meanwhile, managing the core business is termed an "exploit" activity, as the current business is well understood and can be leveraged and mined for efficiencies that further increase its profitability, thereby exploiting the business model. Christensen also suggests that innovation must be treated as an investment, with different hurdles and expectations versus the typical quarterly return on investment (ROI) the exploit business faces. Initial profit relief for explore activity enables the business to experiment, free from stringent internal hurdles that can strangle and prematurely extinguish innovation.

The Innovator's Dilemma and its insights around the explore/exploit approach were groundbreaking and widely heralded. Many companies around the world embraced and adopted the approach to bring disruptive innovation to established organizations. However, despite the disruptive innovation theory's liberating promise to big businesses, still incumbents in establish industries were being disrupted.

It was observed that there were some pitfalls to the model, particularly in cases where the concepts of explore and exploit were misunderstood or mutated over time. Some managers took the word "exploit" literally and started to treat the core business units as cash cows. These business units were what the organization and leaders knew best; they already had mastery of operations, knowledge of customers and clear financial hurdles defining what success looked like. Thus, rather than deliver the incremental, sustaining innovations needed to evolve the offer, they often resorted to cost-cutting and similar activities to exploit the potential for greater ROI. Unfortunately, this salami-slicing of the customer and product experience often had the consequence of actually accelerating the core businesses' decline.

Another pitfall of the model was that sometimes the explore business units lacked the impetus and urgency to practically apply their innovations and realize commercial potential. Explore activities do need to eventually be exploited, yet incubators often struggled to land relevant applications for their innovations. The classic example of this is the famed visit by Steve Jobs to the Xerox PARC technology hub in 1979. Xerox had spun off its innovation to different business units, which were not only financially separate, but also physically separate – based in Silicon Valley, California, close to other tech startups, but far away from Xerox's New York headquarters. During the visit, Jobs encountered the Xerox optical mouse and graphical user interface technology. Despite these being revolutionary technologies, the Xerox PARC team could not imagine any applications for them. Jobs, on the other hand, immediately saw an opportunity for a simplified interface for personal computers that would become the backbone of Apple's friendly and easy-to-use user experience. He negotiated to acquire the technology for a shockingly low value as Xerox did not understand the potential of what it had created.

In 2011, Charles O'Reilly and Michael Tushman, two business and management scholars from Stanford University and Harvard Business School respectively, addressed the pitfalls and challenges of the innovator's dilemma in their 2016 book, *Lead and Disrupt*.[20] The solution they proposed was organizational ambidexterity. Ambidexterity in its purest sense is the ability to use the right and left hands equally well. In the case of solving the innovator's dilemma, it refers to managing the explore/exploit ratio with equal mastery across both sides of the business. This means remaining highly competitive in core markets while also identifying and winning in new spaces. Ambidexterity requires companies to foster multiple contradictory structures, cultures, processes and management in their organizations – no easy feat for even the most skilled and for-ward-thinking of CEOs and still the Achilles heel of many Western businesses today.

So why in a book about China innovation are we talking about classic Harvard Business School innovation theories and well-known stories of dinosaur incumbents disrupted by startups? Because it is important to first capture the challenges most commonly faced by Western businesses in order to understand how Chinese businesses so deftly avoid them.

In China, businesses are almost always naturally ambidex-trous, with equally strong capabilities and commitment put forward

---

20.   Charles O'Reilly, Michael Tushman, *Lead and Disrupt* (California: Stanford Business Books, 2016).

simultaneously on both explore and exploit activities. Chinese businesses also go one step further by connecting the dots to explode the potential of existing technologies by pairing them up with explore activities to magnify the impact of both. In connecting the dots between both the explore and exploit streams, Chinese businesses seem to innately recognize how one area might inform the other. In this way, Chinese businesses are not only ambidextrous, but also ensure that explore and exploit streams periodically intersect, conjoin, and diverge again, having a distinct fluidity that enables yet more dots to be connected. This fluidity of connecting the dots and transferring existing technologies and concepts to new contexts has made Chinese businesses wildly successful, generating massive value creation.

Ambidextrous Innovation at the World's Most Valuable Unicorn

You may have never heard of ByteDance, but you most certainly have heard of its breakthrough product, TikTok. Today, Beijing-based ByteDance is the most valuable startup unicorn in the world, after only 10 years of operation. Valued at over US$350bn[21] at the end of 2021, with 110,000 employees (double the staff of Facebook)[22] and 1.9bn monthly active users across 150 countries and 75 languages[23], ByteDance operates the most popular news app in

21.   Yujie Xue, "ByteDance Overtakes AntGroup as the World's Most Valuable Unicorn", *South China Morning Post*, December 20, 2021. https://www.scmp.com/business/china-business/article/3160424/bytedance-overtakes-ant-group-worlds-most-valuable-unicorn

22.   Roger Chen and Rui Ma, "How ByteDance Became the World's Most Valuable Startup", *Harvard Business Review*, February 24, 2022.

23.   Nessa Anwar, "What is ByteDance?", CNBC, accessed June 8, 2022. https://

China, Toutiao (Today's Headlines), as well as the global sensation short-video social sharing app TikTok, known as Douyin in China. TikTok/Douyin alone has been downloaded 3.3bn[24] times globally, comparable in downloads to the entire Meta group of global companies including Facebook, Instagram, WhatsApp, Messenger and Oculus. ByteDance's founder Zhang Yiming's fortune doubled in 2021 to reach over US$59bn, and this with only 22% ownership of the company, making him the second-richest man in China, ahead of Alibaba founder Jack Ma, who sits at number five.[25]

Unlike the Alibaba conglomerate, which dominates the e-commerce landscape in China, ByteDance has become a global business phenomenon as the first Chinese technology company to experience breakout success worldwide, at a speed that has left the global tech industry reeling. Sheryl Sandberg, formerly COO of Meta Platforms (Facebook and Instagram), expressed competitive concerns over TikTok during her tenure as COO, stating, "They're growing really quickly, they've gotten to bigger numbers faster than we ever did".[26] And in fact in 2022, stocks of Meta Platforms crashed by more than 40% with industry analysts suggesting that TikTok's success was to

www.cnbc.com/2021/11/03/bytedance-founder-zhang-yiming-steps-down-as-chairman-amid-reshuffle.html

24. Pandaily, "TikTok and Sister App Douyin Exceed 3.3 Billion Downloads Worldwide, Generating Nearly 1000 Related Apps", November 25, 2021. https://pandaily.com/tiktok-and-sister-app-douyin-exceed-3-3-billion-downloads-worldwide-generating-near-1000-related-apps/

25. Russell Flannery, "TikTok's Zhang Yiming's Fortune More Than Doubles as the App's Global Popularity Grows", *Forbes*, November 3, 2021. https://www.forbes.com/sites/russellflannery/2021/11/03/tiktoks-zhang-yimings-fortune-more-than-doubles-as-the-apps-global-popularity-grows/?sh=43ef5be23151

26. Isobel Asher Hamilton, "Sheryl Sandberg Says She Worries About TikTok", *Business Insider*, February 27, 2020. https://www.businessinsider.com/sheryl-sandberg-said-she-worries-about-tiktok-2020-2

blame for Meta's poor performance[27]. Meanwhile in China, Chinese businesses are emboldened by ByteDance and TikTok's global success seeing their worldwide expansion as a model to follow. This is why the story of ByteDance is so compelling – and so revealing of the importance of organizational ambidexterity to innovation.

"Explore" Innovation at ByteDance

First, the "explore" innovation of ByteDance is its proprietary technology stack of artificial intelligence (AI) recommendation algorithms and user profiles which combine to deliver highly personalized content. This is markedly different from other social apps, which have historically relied on search or social connections' likes as methods for users to self-select content. ByteDance's apps feed the user personalized content based on a user profile, which is generated from user data – the more the user engages with the app, the smarter the algorithm gets, and the more personalized and relevant the content becomes. This is what makes the TikTok user experience stickier and stickier – some might say even addictive. What is more, this technology stack is a breakthrough that no competitor has yet to match with anything approaching the same results. Facebook tried with Lasso, a TikTok-inspired app, piloted in Mexico in 2018 – but Lasso failed and was off the market by 2020, with fewer than 80,000 daily active users[28].

---

27.   Paul R. La Monica, "It's Been a Rough Year for Social Media Stocks. Blame TikTok", CNN Business, June 8, 2022.

28.   Manish Singh, "Facebook Shutting Down Lasso, It's TikTok Clone", techcrunch.com, July 2, 2020. https://techcrunch.com/2020/07/01/lasso-facebook-tiktok-shut-down/

The irony is that TikTok does not see itself a social app at all, even though this is how the world characterizes it. Rather, Byte-Dance believes TikTok is a content-based community, and founder Zhang often comments that he sees the app as more of a short-video TV platform for the modern mobile age, as opposed to a video-first social media platform. It is no surprise that the orientation of the technology stack is about linking users with content that they will uniquely enjoy. The social component is secondary to the content as the driving feature, but it just so happens that other users, with similar profiles and interests can and do connect. However, the user feed is ultimately highly personalized based on the individual user profile in the app, and what users see is not driven by their social connections' likes or comments. Yet, this technology was not originally developed for short-form video and music at all. It emerged in one of ByteDance's first products, Toutiao, a daily news and information aggregator app in China.

Toutiao was one of ByteDance's first products and was based on insights Zhang gathered from his past experiences. Prior to Toutiao, ByteDance – which at the time was approximately 30 people working in a Beijing apartment – had launched a number of smaller apps in the entertainment space, mainly based on memes. None were particularly successful but with every failure, Zhang accumulated important learnings on what worked, what did not, and what users' pain points were. Also prior to ByteDance, Zhang had worked across a number of Beijing-based startups such as 99fang (real estate app) and Kuxun (travel app), as well as established stalwart Microsoft. Based on all of these experiences, he felt he recognized a set of three unmet needs and pain points that no platform had successfully solved:

1. The small screen of a smartphone and the resulting limitations for mobile browsing.
2. Users' fragmented time, such that the moments when they wanted to browse – a few minutes in a queue or waiting for the bus – were so short as to limit their ability to engage with typical content formats.
3. Information overload of news, entertainment and social media, such that it was not easy to navigate to the content most suitable for them.[29]

Zhang decided to solve these needs using a news and information platform, on the basis that news is something people look at even if they only have 1 minute and because staying informed is a basic human need. But he also wanted to go one step further and design a platform that would serve as a personal recommendation engine by using big data and machine learning to understand users.

At the time, in 2012, using AI to curate news was a radical concept. News was a business where information was curated by human editors – it was individuals who decided which stories were "big" and which were not. The original news platform and the model for all others was the Yahoo portal. But in fact, this model was merely the existing model of news overlaid on the technology of the internet. News was not "personalized" other than if a user indicated they preferred to see world news over local news, or sports over business. For most users, news was still search-based – if they wanted to read about a current event, they would search for it on Yahoo or Google, or in the case of China, they used the search engine Baidu. But

---

29.   Michael Brennan, *Attention Factory* (Independently Published, October 10, 2020).

Zhang imagined a product that would shift this dynamic. Instead of people looking for information, he imagined information looking for people. By moving from search to recommendation, he would remove the need for the user to take specific actions. Spotting this opportunity was the key to Zhang disrupting the news and information industry by leveraging the underutilized power of the channel to serve users better, providing a customized product that delivered greater convenience and better outcomes.

The Toutiao user profile is key to hyper-personalization. It comprises three types of data[30] that Zhang felt would most accurately capture the information needed to deliver highly relevant content to each individual user. First, there is user data, including demographic information such as age and gender, as well as type of device, browsing history, etc. Second, content data is gathered, which includes the typical catalogue of content the user engages with. Third is environment data, such as where the user is, the stability of their network, home versus workplace, whether they are on public transport, what the weather is like at their location.

Toutiao then applies machine learning to anticipate user tastes. Two key processes are used: (1) content-based filtering, which offers recommendations to users based on past content viewed; and (2) collaborative filtering, which builds group profiles of users who enjoy similar types of content and uses one user as a proxy to serve the content to the others.[31] Content is then optimized based on what the user might like to read, which gives the content a "recommendation value" score. Likes, clickthroughs and completion rate increase the recommendation value, whereas short reading time decreases it.

---

30.   Brennan, *Attention Factory*.
31.   Brennan, *Attention Factory*.

The recommendation value of content also decreases over time as information goes out of date. With every click or hover, the data network effect takes over as the algorithm gets smarter, the user profile becomes more robust, understanding more and more what content users prefer. With a better user experience, users are more engaged, spending more time in the app, which further enriches the user profile, which creates even better content matching, and so on....

With 45%[32] user retention rates in Toutiao in 2012, one of the highest ever seen globally at that time, Zhang knew he was on to something big. By creating the filtering processes and user profiles and combining them, Zhang had successfully innovated to create an AI-driven growth flywheel that set a new standard for personalization and could be an engine for any type of user platform and a game-changing technology disruptor for ByteDance.

With this flywheel, Zhang realised that ByteDance could become an app factory. All they needed to do was identify unique app concepts with a supporting content model and apply the content-plus-personalization flywheel. And further, as apps go in and out of fashion, it did not matter if some failed, because the information generated by the technology stack could still be used to enrich user profiles and improve the recommendation engine across all apps, making current and potential new apps stickier and stickier. Finally, Zhang believed this flywheel transcended culture, which would give him the opportunity to explore a global super app – a feat never achieved by a Chinese company. With 80% of the world's internet users outside of China,[33] the biggest opportunities were in overseas markets. But successful global apps typically relied on

---

32.   Brennan, *Attention Factory.*
33.   Brennan, *Attention Factory.*

some cultural adaptation and human curation when moving overseas, which had prevented many Chinese apps from becoming global, with the fixed cost of product development for new markets being high. But Zhang felt the growth flywheel reduced the need for large-scale adaptation and human curation, as with AI as the engine, the user profiles themselves acted to naturally adapt the app – so the cost of serving an incremental user for ByteDance would be close to zero.

This realization led to Zhang breaking off several teams from the main business to experiment with what these new global apps could be. These teams still enjoyed the resources of the larger business – for example engineering, programming, or legal support – but they were relieved of profit and ROI pressures or seeking investment, giving them an advantage over independent startups, who had to balance both financing and development. Under this operating structure, the teams were encouraged to undertake systematic experimentation to find the world's next super app. Zhang felt that a news and information app from China would be too politically sensitive, so Toutiao was not going to be the main candidate for becoming a global super app; instead, he had a sense that there could be something in the space of entertainment that could be.

ByteDance finally hit gold a couple of years later by exploring learnings from the still successful and growing Toutiao. In 2015, with Toutiao having revolutionized the news and information game in China, overall content on the internet and apps had also evolved globally thanks to smartphones and 4G connectivity, with short-form video emerging as a new, highly engaging form of content. On Toutiao, Zhang observed that short video content (6–15 seconds long) was stickier than any other content, and he wondered if this could lead to a new platform for ByteDance. He also saw new short-video, music-driven platforms like Vine (US), Musical.ly (China-based, with users in US and EU) and Kuaishou (China) taking off with young, trendy users. So, he tasked an incubation team of 10 employees (from the now 2,000-strong business of Toutiao) to explore short-form video, giving them the simple brief to explore "mobile TV for the world[34]" using the ByteDance flywheel.

Douyin and TikTok were born from this incubator and soon launched across China and Japan. Having a need for initial user profiles, ByteDance acquired local apps in India and Indonesia to gain entry points. Subsequently it acquired Musical.ly, the China-based app with a small following in the US and Europe, for the same purpose. And the rest, as they say, is history.

ByteDance Delivers Exploit Innovation with Growth Hacking

Aside from exploiting the personalization flywheel across platforms to create an app factory, how did ByteDance and Douyin/TikTok apply "exploit" principles to drive growth, revenue and profitability?

In Chinese tech startups at this time, digital marketing was not as developed as in the US. In the US, tech startups scaled their platforms by relying on sizable, data-driven sales and digital marketing budgets to spread the word and acquire users. Chinese tech companies, on the other hand, relied on operations departments to scale growth by interacting in low-tech, low-cost ways with all actors across the value chain, a practice known as growth hacking, which takes the shape of hands-on activities by the operations team with a single goal – to achieve massive growth on a slim budget.

---

34. Brennan, *Attention Factory*.

Growth hacking is low-tech enterprise for any business in any industry, but it seems especially low-tech when compared with the leading-edge proprietary technology in ByteDance's tech stack. Douyin/TikTok focused on exploiting creative, resource-light and generally budget-minded ways to acquire users. Marketing and operational practices that showed promise on a small scale were then more fully exploited with increasing levels of investment to scale the activity and scale growth. Very few of these were new ideas; rather, ByteDance was exploiting learnings from other start-ups' experiences in growth hacking:

- From the very beginning, Douyin/TikTok allowed users to create and export videos to be posted on any and all social platforms. These videos contained a Douyin/TikTok water-mark and the user's ID, which helped to promote the app and the user simultaneously.
- Every member of the business, including CEO Zhang, were required to create their own accounts and own content, with specific goals and KPIs for views.
- The ByteDance team also set up accounts across other social media platforms like Weibo and WeChat in China, Facebook and Instagram globally, and posted their own watermarked videos to spread awareness of the brand and technology.
- In China, ByteDance set up a cross-conversion system leveraging their other popular apps to migrate users to Douyin. These self-owned acquisition channels were espe-cially cost-effective, with the cost estimated at US$0.016 per user.[35]

---

35. Brennan, *Attention Factory.*

- ByteDance even created other apps to use as cheap recruitment tools. Meme apps, for example, helped to identify entertainment-seeking users and funnel them to Douyin.

- The Douyin operations team took note of "super users" who were deeply engaged with the app and invited them to lunch to get their advice, co-creating and guiding the evolution of the user experience. This led to additions of features like appearance-altering filters, which allow content creators to look more professional and even film without applying makeup, thus removing the friction from content creation.

- Globally, the operations team set up promotional accounts and ran in-app advertising on other platforms, cleverly employing historical figures to create talent-fee-free campaign memes that went viral, e.g., Mona Lisa or Abraham Lincoln lip-syncing or using the app.

- In China, where the practice was allowed at the time, ByteDance paid US$0.06 per mobile device[36] to have Douyin pre-installed on Android phones by distributors, removing the need to download and increasing the likelihood of potential users trying out the app.

- Globally, knowing that the app experience was sticky and had a high retention rate, ByteDance removed barriers to trial/adoption by allowing users to experience the app without having to commit through a registration process. They were able to still deliver a high degree of personalization by creating a shadow profile of the user based on device ID and physical location to serve relevant content.

---

36. Brennan, *Attention Factory*.

- Douyin engaged China's urban youth by sponsoring a hip-hop talent show, "The Rap of China", which was also able to generate free high-value short-video content for the app.
- In Asia, where "promoter girls" are used to flog everything from ice teas to mobile phone minutes, ByteDance deployed attractive female university students as Douyin promoters. These promoters stood in high-traffic areas giving out small gifts or cash for those that would install the app on their phone. This was reported to lead to a strong proportion of older male users joining the app, which also served to answer the goal of "aging up" the short-video format beyond its existing user base of pre-teens/teens at the time.
- In China and globally, Douyin/TikTok set up challenges to give users added motivation to produce as well as a framework to make content creation simple. The challenges often went viral and across platforms beyond Douyin and took over social media globally.
- With local content being a key ingredient in the success in each market, the most significant spends were used to subsidize content creators, oftentimes with strong creators even having account managers from the platform to help them optimize their content and grow their followings. To source creators, Douyin/TikTok often targeted art schools and art students to get more unique and creative content. Globally, they brought creators together for exclusive parties which not only rewarded the creators but also had the effect of generating more content for the platform.

By Q1 2018, Douyin/TikTok was the world's most downloaded app[37], and by 2020 enjoyed the highest retention rates in China in the industry at close to 90%.[38] There were even people on YouTube creating videos about TikTok videos, with many of these being 10 minutes long and garnering millions of views themselves. To create "a Douyin" or "a TikTok" became common parlance in the internet world for creating a short video. Douyin/TikTok was taking over the culture of the internet.

A concurrent challenge was how to monetize the app as user momentum was building. Growth hacking methods, often borrowed from other tech industries, were used to drive revenue. One such tool for monetization, inspired by computer gaming, was in-app purchases of virtual coins. Users can buy TikTok Coins with real money and buy things in the app like emojis as well as "gifts" or "diamonds" to give to their favourite content creators as tips in appreciation for the content. If the creator wishes to cash in their gifts or diamonds for real money, the app takes 50% of this as commission. From June 2018 to May 2020, the platform experienced 4,233% revenue growth in in-app purchases, and in 2022, revenue was estimated to be US$78m.[39]

Advertising is, by far, the largest contributor to the platform's revenue. Using the same personalization engine as for content, TikTok/Douyin can deliver extremely targeted messages, which has made it a go-to app for digital marketing and advertisers such

---

37.   Brennan, *Attention Factory*.
38.   Thomas Graziani, "Douyin, Kuaishou, Bilibili, Red: Where to Promote Your Brand in China Besides WeChat", Jing Daily, May 14, 2020. https://jingdaily.com/douyin-kuaishou-red-bilibili-where-to-promote-your-brand-in-china-besides-wechat/
39.   Tristan Rose, "How Does TikTok Make Money?", entrepreneur-360.com, April 8, 2022. https://entrepreneur-360.com/how-does-tiktok-make-money-12356

as Coca-Cola, the NBA, The Washington Post, Apple, BMW and Marvel, to name just a few. It is the main revenue engine for the app and is such a popular channel for digital marketing that Douyin/ TikTok was projected to comprise 5.3% of the total global digital ad market at $31.66bn in sales in 2022.[40] It was estimated that nearly 40% of the employees were sales staff,[41] who not only sell ad space but advise advertisers on content. Advertising often looks like – and to some degree *is* – another form of content, taking the shape of video challenges, entertaining content and hashtags that go viral. This type of advertising content performs better than other channels for the advertiser as it is more enjoyable and thus more watched by the target audience than traditional product-presentation advertising. Combine this with the precision of the personalization engine and Douyin/TikTok is reported to be a preferred channel due to both efficiency and effectiveness for advertisers.

Another significant component of revenue (since 2020) is e-commerce sales. By adding e-commerce functionality to the app, so that users can buy items they see in the videos, Douyin/TikTok essentially pioneered a new social selling tool, now known as social commerce. In year one, total sales were US$119bn from social commerce on Douyin, and by 2022, this is expected to increase to US$180bn, a growth of 35%.[42]

---

40.   Sara Lebow, "TikTok and Douyin Will Account for More Than 5% of Global Digital Ad Spend This Year", *EMarketer.com*, April 13, 2022. https://emarketer.com/content/tiktok-douyin-digital-ad-spend

41.   Brennan, *Attention Factory.*

42.   Emma Lee, "Douyin Sees Ecommerce Sales More Than Tripled in the Past Year", Technode.com, June 1, 2022. https://technode.com/2022/06/01/douyin-sees-e-commerce-sales-more-than-tripled-in-the-past-year/

Ambidextrous Operations at ByteDance

ByteDance's success as an app factory, with now 21 successful apps in China and globally, can be attributed not only to the tech stack which includes the personalization flywheel, but also the way that the company has created workstreams that are separate, but with shared services as well as strategic points of intersection so that all the workstreams or ventures may inform and ultimately advance one another.

While shared service platforms (SSPs) are not a new concept, the innovative way ByteDance makes use of its SSP is.[43] When small venture teams, usually only with a handful of people, are put together to explore new innovations, they look to the SSP for all needed operating resources. In other companies, SSPs typically consist of legal, HR, IT and sales, but at ByteDance, the tech stack – led by engineering, programming and user-research – is at the heart of the SSP. When the venture teams are seeking to solve unmet user needs, they can tap into the SSP to accelerate the process. User-research specialists provide market analysis, often already existing from previous or concurrent projects. Engineers provide the programming for new products or features, often off the shelf in their internal archive, tweaked for the new use cases. Shared operational tools and a cloud, developed in-house, enable ByteDance to efficiently operate the SSP, with all information and operating resources readily available. Venture teams need only tap into the SSP and they can fly through rapid iterations to arrive at a product in a fraction of the time it takes their competitors. For comparison, ByteDance launched an education app in only four months, a feat

---

43. Chen and Ma, "How ByteDance Became the World's Most Valuable Startup".

that industry experts speculated would have taken competitors at least 18 months.[44]

The cost of exploration is marginal as teams are small and nimble and draw on the SSP. Therefore, ByteDance does not mind having multiple teams exploring the same space. There are very few redundancies in the system, which enables ByteDance to launch 12 entertainment apps in a single year as well as have more than 20 concurrent projects exploring overseas expansion.[45] On the flip side, ByteDance dissolves non-performing venture teams with speed, being able to identify quickly what has potential and what does not. This has the effect of enabling the company to cycle through a greater number of exploratory ventures annually compared to their competitors, which is a significant competitive advantage in the fast-moving tech industry.

Venture teams are not just used to develop new products, but also to identify new trajectories for growth with existing products, including user acquisition, innovating content or features, or even new advertising products for increased monetization. In this way, the SSP is used to supercharge both incremental innovation and exploitation of the existing business model, making ByteDance apps better and better for users and more profitable for the business, creating a virtuous cycle of exploit activities, including incremental innovation for existing products. Add this to the AI-driven personalization flywheel that drives explore activities and innovation and you have seemingly perfect ambidexterity. Explore and exploit activities are in harmonious balance and each workstream informs the others, enabling the organization to successfully connect the dots

---

44.   Chen and Ma, "How ByteDance Became the World's Most Valuable Startup".
45.   Chen and Ma, "How ByteDance Became the World's Most Valuable Startup".

between explore and exploit to realize potential. It is no wonder ByteDance is the world's most valuable startup.

How to Export This Catalyst

Chinese businesses adroitly solve the innovator's dilemma with managerial ambidexterity of explore and exploit, layered with certain characteristics that are unique to Chinese business. While a deep dive into tech innovator ByteDance is employed here as a detailed illustration, this type of Chinese-style ambidexterity is readily observed in many industries and types of businesses, not just startups and not just tech. So how do businesses achieve this more readily in China and what strategies can Western businesses export to increase their own ambidexterity?

Embrace Change as the Only Constant

Even the largest organizations in China display an incredible ability to morph. Unlike large corporates in the West, which often operate like large ocean tankers, taking considerable time to chart new courses and slowly steer to the new path, large corporates in China pivot nimbly. There is a spirit of entrepreneurship in even the biggest companies, and one rarely hears comments like "This is how we have always done it" or "We tried that before". There are no fixtures or certainties; everything is open to be challenged, questioned, and changed.

Due to the amount of progress the culture has witnessed in China, the entire population is largely accepting of change. In the West, this kind of openness to progress is generally only seen with younger generations. However, in China, even people in the latter part of their working years show amazing flexibility in the face of change. In his book, *Young China*, Zak Dychtwald identifies this critical cultural distinction as a significant competitive advantage for China versus the West. Dychtwald describes the people of China as "hundreds of millions of hyper-adoptive and hyper-adaptive consumers...and on that front China has no peer".[46]

A hyper-adaptive culture is a critical precondition for businesses to Chinafy. While startups have the luxury of creating this kind of environment from the beginning, established organizations must unlearn deeply entrenched values. This means the organization must shed obsolete mental models, conventional approaches to R&D, and potentially revisit or abandon current business models. To Chinafy, companies must focus on building an internal culture with strong change values, recruiting "citizens" who display openness to being a part of an organization that embraces – and ideally, rewards – flexibility and adaptation to changing circumstances. This means recruiting differently for employees who are more predisposed to a culture where disruptive growth is a priority, screening out those who are likely to be unwilling to challenge convention. It may mean changing processes, removing system rigidity, or even revisiting strategies that are valued because they served the company in the past.

Given the amount of change, this is not the stuff of managers, it is the stuff of CEOs and leaders. Cultural change starts at the top and must trickle down, infusing every corner of the organization.

---

46. Zak Dychtwald, "China's New Innovation Advantage", *Harvard Business Review,* May-June 2021 issue.

Have a Strong Reason Why

A strong "reason why" linked to strategic intent provides a clear and compelling logic for working towards the desired outcomes. This is required to justify shifts in ways of working. Otherwise, there is no drive for employees to share information transparently, behave collaboratively, or for managers to sacrifice resources to fund small, uncertain explore activities. This is because, when under pressure, manager tend to hold on to their resources and drive their own outcomes. Managers routinely discount future threats and are more oriented to the quarterly gains that stakeholders heap praise upon them for.

Ambidexterity needs to become part of the fabric of the organization, part of its identity. If there is no shared purpose or "reason why" to behave ambidextrously, it is incredibly easy for employees to revert to comfortable past behaviours. Gaining commitment around a simple, clear "reason why" is something Chinese companies are particularly good at, although it's not solely the province of Chinese companies. It generally starts with a clear vision communicated from the very top. In the case of ByteDance, this was Zhang Yiming's focused purpose of turning the search paradigm on its head and helping information find people. We know Jack Ma as the leader of the Alibaba Group whose vision was to open the world's eyes to China's wealth of export goods. In the US, there is also Elon Musk and his mission to build the world's first colony on Mars.

The bottom line is, if you have an organization you need to shift, it is not going to be possible without a compelling reason why the current way of working must change. Until you make it a "must", it will likely be a "should", a "could", or "let's try". This leaves your business in limbo, operating in a grey area between your previous and your future organization, and unable to deliver either mission well. For startups, a compelling "reason why" becomes the jumping-off platform for your business, which will shape everything your company does. In either case, an ambitious yet focused "reason why" is the starting point. Without this, the organization will stumble.

Dynamically Seize Opportunities

A key difference between Chinese and Western companies is often referred to as "China speed". The term is typically used to describe manufacturing agility. However, China speed manifests across all dimensions of business, but perhaps in no one area as clearly as seizing opportunities. Chinese businesses do not hesitate to deploy resources at the spark of an idea to explore its potential. Small "skunkworks" teams are assembled quickly, with resources allocated to explore the opportunity. These dynamic capabilities form a kind of sustained competitive advantage for Chinese businesses and enable firms to assemble and reconfigure resources – a kind of operational flexibility and fitness. To Chinafy, businesses must exercise and strengthen this muscle in their own organizations.

Connect the Dots

Western businesses must expand upon the principles of ambidextrous management and go one step further to enable a fluidity and intersection of both explore and exploit activities. With constant sharing and cross-pollination across explore/exploit lanes, it is possible to connect the dots between the two streams more readily and leverage the iterative learnings meaningfully across the entire business. This often leads to a new type of innovation which we can think of as "application innovation", which is particularly strong in Chinese companies – it is when existing, under-leveraged assets or technologies find their way into new impactful innovation applications.

Chinese businesses often have different ways of organizing and working that maximize sharing and cross-pollination of ideas. These different ways of working aggregate into a distinct and uniquely Chinese type of management strategy and business culture unto itself, which leads to a high propensity for application innovations. Perhaps the most critical difference is that Chinese companies often take high-value processes and make them shared services, rather than lower-value administrative processes like HR or legal.

The explore function sits at the centre of the organization to be fully maximized and exploited by working teams – taking Byte-Dance's tech-engine as SSP as an example. Project teams are small and focused and can tap into the explore function as needed, making them incredibly nimble. They can pull technologies off the shelf or brief in the spec for a totally new technology to the SSP. CEO-level and C-suite management have a strong focus on organizational structure and information flows, ensuring that the organization is not only collecting the dots, but also connecting them to create new-to-the-world innovations as well as uncover exciting application innovations. Culturally, information is data-driven, open and available, widely shared and reviewed in cross-functional forums, because any one data point, failed algorithm on another project, or user insight could spawn a new innovation for a different project team.

The smaller the company, the more challenging it is to ambidextrously manage both explore and exploit, as it can be like juggling between the present and the future – a daunting task for any organization and even more so for those that are resource-constrained. However, one can see from the ByteDance case that it is possible. What is now the world's most valuable startup was once a handful of people operating ambidextrously in an apartment in Beijing. What is key for small businesses is managing the explore-exploit ratio (E:E). The E:E balance is fundamental to ensuring business is continually operating in two modes and not prioritizing one at the expense of the other.

The challenge can be that exploitation is often more readily understood and straightforward, with faster outcomes than the explore side. This creates a temptation, especially in small businesses – which necessarily have an eye to short-term results that generate cash flow – to lean more heavily into exploit activities. Another equal and opposite tension in small businesses is that entrepreneurs tend to be more visionary and risk-taking, and thus tend to be magnetically drawn to exploring big ideas and innovation and lose sight of the exploit opportunities. This is why small businesses should explicitly state, measure and track the E:E ratio as a goal to avoid falling into either of these traps.

Organize Horizontally

To Chinafy, organizational structures are often flat, leaving people to focus on delivering their responsibilities rather dealing with the complexity of managing stakeholders. This gives the organization a horizontal flexibility, which allows them to assemble and recombine resources quickly and easily and keeps the teams focused on problem-solving for the opportunity at hand. As we can see with ByteDance, teams may even have a degree of overlap in their scope, but this enables full yet nimble coverage with a variety of perspectives brought to bear on high-potential opportunities. In this way, the disruption in the business model is that Chinese R&D employs more of a "creation" process as opposed to the "discovery" process which is more widely used by Western companies.

Horizontal flexibility makes Chinese businesses wildly more productive, launching as many as 20 new innovations for the same cost as one innovation from their Western counterparts.[47] As each innovation represents a small bet, it means that failures are less costly and detrimental to the overall organization and only a few of these innovations need to become big wins. As a result, companies can be more experimental, more risk-taking, launching products early and in beta for iterative improvement insights with a reduced pressure for generating payback on the investment. This combination makes Chinese companies more agile, able to seize and capture opportunity and value more readily.

Flat organizations with horizontal flexibility tend to require more upfront alignment and accountability in outcomes. A system commonly used in China to drive alignment and accountability is the Objectives and Key Results (OKR) system. This is not a uniquely Chinese system. It is employed by many Western organizations like Google and Amazon as well as Chinese companies like ByteDance. Leaders all over the world find OKR systems a highly effective tool to align the larger strategic objectives of the company with the day-to-day actions and output of employees – because as the saying goes, "What gets measured, gets managed."

Strategy and operations both under an OKR system creates a transparent and clear dashboard allowing both managers and employees to have equal hands in managing businesses ambidextrously. All goals are visible in the organization, at every level, which not only helps everyone pull in the same direction but also

---

47.   Feng Wan, Peter Williamson, et al. "Antecedents and Implications of Disruptive Innovation: Evidence from China", *Technovation: The International Journal of Technological Innovation, Entrepreneurship and Technology Management*, May 2014 issue.

demonstrates when certain teams might need help or support – its most important contribution being that in doing so it eliminates siloed thinking. OKRs enable the teams to see the correlations between one team's outcomes and another's, which drives a more collaborative environment overall, generating more fluidity and intersections of valuable information, thus ultimately more and better outcomes. Much like a startup's flywheel, an OKR system gets stronger, smarter, and more fit for purpose with continued use.

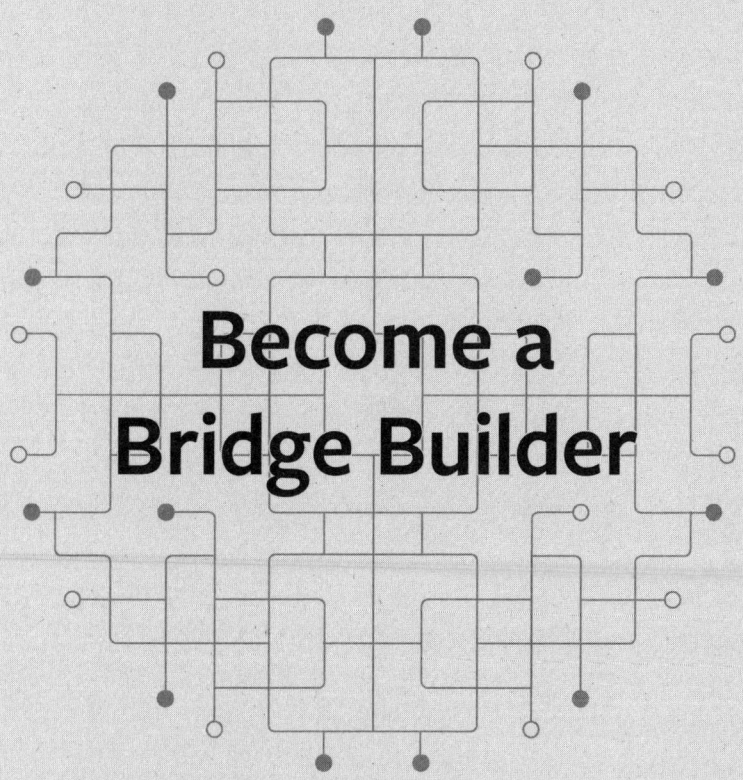

Chapter 4

Become a
Bridge Builder

CATALYST 2

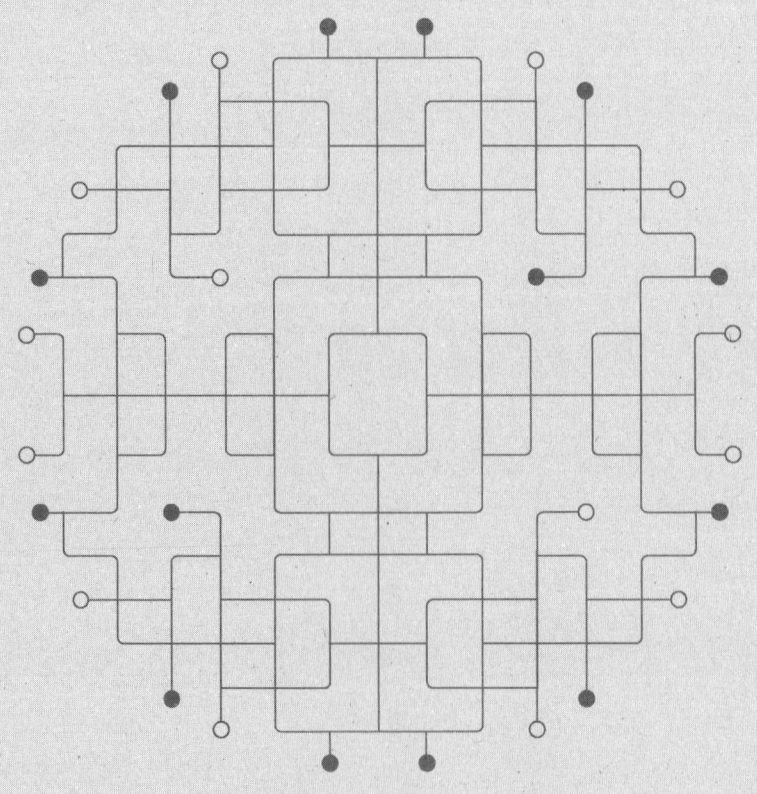

THERE IS OFTEN a lag time between invention and its widespread adoption into the mainstream. This can be months for some innovations and years or even decades for others. For example, it took more than 60 years for cloud storage to become adopted into the mainstream.

Cloud storage is believed to have been invented by computer scientist Dr J.C.R. Licklider in the 1960s. It was only in the 1980s that CompuServe began to offer its customers small amounts of disk space to store some of their files, but even 20 years later the service was not widely utilized. What prevented cloud storage from taking off?

For starters, personal computers were not widely used at the time. In general, there was much less information to manage than we have today. Record-keeping, documents and data were largely analogue, not digital. While large global companies might have had a need for the management of and easy access to large amounts of information, there was no such need for smaller operations or individuals. Further, cloud storage was complex to use and access, requiring trained staff for operations. It was only in the 2020s that cloud storage entered mainstream usage, and there are still barriers to its further propagation, including unreliable internet speeds in a great many places in the world, as well as rising concerns regarding privacy and security globally.

What is needed to reduce the lag time between invention and adoption is often *enabling innovations* – innovations around the core innovation that close the gap between the innovation's birth and its entry into the mainstream. Think of these enablers as bridges – bridging any barriers to use that would otherwise prevent the core invention or innovation from propagating.

Consider the simple example of bridge building. In the 1800s steam engine trains were an invention that represented a massive leap forward for society in terms of mobility. However, trains themselves could only propagate as a means of transport with tracks to drive them on, drivers who could operate them, and ticketing systems and depots to manage passengers and journeys. The invention of the train could have had relatively low impact if not for the enabling infrastructure and service innovations that allowed trains to become a dominant mode of transport.

The most successful innovators build bridges to accelerate the adoption of innovation, reducing the lag time between invention and impact – and this is an area where China particularly excels. Chinese businesses recognize that technology or invention rarely drives change on its own; for innovation to spread, businesses must be proactive in creating complementary assets to remove barriers and build bridges for mass adoption.

Chinese company Alibaba used this strategy successfully to accelerate the explosion of e-commerce with an enabling innovation – the Alipay digital payment system – making both a pervasive part of everyday Chinese life.

Alibaba Builds a Bridge for E-commerce

Jack Ma, in his job as a Chinese-to-English translator, travelled to the US in 1995 as part of an economic delegation with his employer, the Hangzhou municipal government. There he saw the power of the

Internet as a tool for business and decided to explore its potential in China. Ma's vision was to share the wide variety of China-made goods with the world – via the internet.

After a few attempts, this finally took the shape of Alibaba in 1999, a business-to-business (B2B) website where small to medium sized Chinese businesses could connect and sell their goods to international buyers. Alibaba's company name was inspired by the Persian folk stories of *One Thousand and One Nights*, featuring the character, Ali Baba. With this story being internationally known, Ma believed the company name Alibaba could be easily understood by people from many countries and represent a secret password – the equivalent of "open sesame" – opening China and Chinese goods to the world. Even the Alibaba logo was inspired by the same story, assuming the form of Aladdin's magic lamp.

Yet, in 1999 in China, internet penetration was less than 1% of the population – much less when compared to the US at 36%[48] at the time. Ma chose a B2B approach out of necessity. But even for his B2B Chinese sellers, Ma and his team had to build the websites for these customers to have a storefront on Alibaba.com. It was an investment for those sellers who paid around US$2,500 to have their websites on Alibaba built, but as pioneers in this space, the investment easily paid off – and usually in the first order. As word spread of Alibaba's success in opening the market for Chinese goods overseas, more and more sellers joined and Alibaba gained momentum.

While trading directly with small to medium businesses in China was new for many international buyers, the constructs of trading, including methods of payment and transaction, were not.

---

48.   World Bank historical data, accessed July 20, 2022. https://data.worldbank.org/indicator/IT.NET.USER.ZS?locations=CN

In the world of B2B trading, minimum order quantity, wholesale pricing and terms, purchase orders, and payment by bank transfer within 30 to 90 days of receipt of goods, were all commonly accepted ways of working. As such, transactions flowed smoothly between buyers and sellers with the constructs and paradigms of trust enabled by the frameworks existing in global B2B business.

However, when Ma sought to launch Taobao in 2003, the Amazon-meets-eBay of China, this was not the case with everyday consumers. While Internet usage was growing in China, still only 1% of the Chinese population were shopping online.[49] And it would not be until 2007 when the Chinese government launched its first e-commerce development scheme[50] that any significant weight would be put behind this channel's development. Thus in 2003, Chinese consumers had no available methods or frames of reference for transacting online, which was a key hindrance in Ma's vision for B2C and C2C e-commerce.

In fact, in the early 2000s, banking was a very simple system in China. While many people held bank accounts to store cash, there was an absence of financial products to manage cash or facilitate payment of any type other than person-to-person transactions. Paying someone, say paying your landlord the monthly rent, was a bank transfer as cheques and debit cards did not exist. Further, online banking did not exist, so to arrange any transaction, it was necessary to go to the bank and either wait in line (usually taking half of a day) or use an in-house terminal or ATM in person (faster, but not intuitive, thus requiring the support of a bank employee).

---

49.   Julie Wulf, "Alibaba Group", *Harvard Business School Case Study*, April 26, 2010.
50.   Xinhua News Press Release, "20 Years of the Internet in China", April 20, 2014. http://www.china.org.cn/business/2014-04/20/content_32150035.htm

Even in the mid-2000s credit cards were uncommon and only held by those who could secure them with proof of automobile or home ownership. And there seemed to be little future for the expansion of credit cards since Chinese society did not value the ability to buy on credit. Culturally, debt (good or bad) was perceived as unacceptable – so much so that not even mortgages were common. Thus, there was no banking industry commitment to develop the infrastructure to facilitate card-based payments.

With anything other than simple, face-to-face cash transactions being exceedingly troublesome, lack of payment options was the main barrier for transactions outside of those directly at the point-of-purchase with cash. This gap in banking and payments was a massive stumbling block for any potential e-commerce enterprise.

Neither Alibaba nor Ma had any express interest, knowledge or experience in personal finance or banking as a business. Alibaba was already a successful global B2B e-commerce platform; yet, to become a consumer-facing e-commerce pioneer in China, the gap in digital payments would have to be tackled. Consumers could not and would not place orders online as they could not easily make payment and even if they did make the payment (via bank transfer), there was no sense of security that the purchased goods would be received. This gap in payments meant that if Ma wanted to see his Taobao B2C enterprise work, he would have to foster enabling innovations – building a bridge between consumers and banks.

With the creation of Alipay, Alibaba created a shadow bank.[51] A shadow bank is a non-regulated financial intermediary that essentially facilitates the creation of credit in the financial system.

---

51. Sara Tsu, "The Rise and Fall of Shadow Banking in China", *The Diplomat*, November 19, 2015.

Alibaba's mechanism as a shadow bank created user accounts that were directly linked to bank accounts, thus effectively enabling remote banking transactions. Payment was further facilitated by QR codes unique to each user or business, which could be transmitted as images by text, email, or chat to be scanned for real-time payment. Alipay also addressed issues of transaction trust by holding funds in escrow for seven days until the buyer confirmed receipt of the product. This enabling innovation was designed solely to bridge Alibaba's expansion into B2C e-commerce but was also more broadly transformative for the Chinese consumer landscape, and in fact became the spark that would ignite the entire Chinese consumer digital economy.

Given the high retail fragmentation in China, unless one lived in a first-tier megacity, many brands and products were unavailable due to the lack of retail infrastructure. The growth of e-commerce, enabled by Alipay, effectively negated the need to expand brick-and-mortar retail stores and rendered the high cost of building the supply chains and distribution networks to service store expansion unnecessary. As such, in pioneering the enabling commercial innovation of digital payments, Alipay enabled a new breed of e-commerce business model in China providing near universal access to Chinese consumers for goods and services, regardless of whether one lived in a megacity like Shanghai or Beijing, or in a rural village.

Despite China's Alipay and US Apple Pay launching in the same year in 2014, China exploded digital payment systems to completely transform China into a cashless society in a way that the US did not. Today, China is over 500 times greater in total expenditures on mobile payment versus the world's leading economy of the US. Rarely do any of its citizens handle cash, credit cards or other physical forms of transaction, as payment is made almost exclusively on mobile devices, with Alipay as the dominant provider. And Alipay continues to innovate. In 2019, it launched a facial recognition payment method, where users can either scan a QR code with a phone or simply use their faces to pay – making digital payment even more frictionless. Alibaba Group now also dominates global e-commerce sales, creating the world's largest shopping day, China's Singles Day 11/11, with sales reaching US$139bn in 2021[52], compared to US$9bn for Black Friday sales in the same year.[53]

Alibaba's enabling innovation of Alipay unlocked an unprecedented wave of digitalized consumerism in China in both speed and scale. Today in China there are approximately 1bn internet users with nearly 30m new users joining each year – that is more than the combined populations of the US, Indonesia and Brazil, three of the world's largest countries[54]. Of China's internet users, 98% access the internet through a mobile phone, 80% have made an online purchase, and 72% of these use digital mobile payment methods.[55] Alipay now enjoys 1.3bn active users globally across 10 countries, compared to approximately 500m active users of Apple Pay globally across more than 70 countries.[56]

52. Arjun Kharpal, "China Singles Day 2021, Record Sales", cnbc.com, November 11, 2021. https://www.cnbc.com/2021/11/12/china-singles-day-2021-alibaba-jd-hit-record-139-billion-of-sales.html
53. Ashley Capoot, "Black Friday Sales top $9B in New Record", cnbc.com, November 26, 2021.
54. HSBC Global Market Reports, "Five Reasons why China is Dominating E-commerce", 2018.
55. HSBC Global Market Reports, "Five Reasons".
56. Rita Liao, "Jack Ma's Fintech Giant Tops 1.3 Billion Users Globally", techcrunch.com, July 15, 2020. https://techcrunch.com/2020/07/14/ant-alibaba-1-3-billion-users/

Social Commerce

Social commerce is flourishing and accelerating at a pace in China that is not seen anywhere else in the world. It is expected to reach $475bn by 2023, comprising more than 14% of China's total e-commerce sales – which is more than 15 times the size of social commerce sales in the US.[57] This disproportionate growth can be attributed to a business model that has utilized enabling innovations to build bridges for a truly frictionless buying experience. By leveraging existing innovations such as e-commerce functionality, livestreaming and group-buying and bolting them onto social, Chinese tech companies have created an entirely new and intoxicating entertainment and shopping universe.

In the West, social commerce is at its core a supply-driven model that exists on a social network[58] – a network where friends connect with one another and where brands and sellers have a platform to deploy an advertising business model to push product information and content to shape the buying decisions of potential consumers. Purchasing typically happens on an external website which requires several critical actions for the consumer to take – they must click through from the social network to the website, potentially navigate the website to find the desired item, add the item to a cart, and add in their shipping, billing and payment details, and finally click to buy.

Chinese social commerce has innovated the model to be a demand model within a social group.[59] The app gathers consumers but does not rely on individual networking or connections as a

---

57. Jason Davis, "Social Commerce: How Pinduoduo and Instagram Challenge Alibaba and Amazon in Ecommerce", INSEAD Case Study, 2020.
58. Davis, "Social Commerce".
59. Davis, "Social Commerce".

starting point. The app's primary draw is informative and entertaining thematic content geared towards certain target audiences and their interests, e.g., fashion and beauty, news and information, etc. This also happens to capture a focused and high potential group of consumers to brands and sellers. Individuals join the app – they can connect with each other, or not, but the experience is enhanced through social connections. The enabling innovation is embedding e-commerce into social, and activating it with dynamic functionality such as livestreaming sales, which brings consumers directly to sellers for a completely frictionless shopping user experience – an experience that is often gamified and is entertaining as well as socially connected for the consumer. Purchasing is typically completed in the social app in as few as two clicks – the first click to select the desired item, the second click to authorize in-app payment. While there is advertising in the app, the business model is dominated by commissions from e-commerce sales that are supercharged by livestream selling events hosted by celebrities and influencers.

Xiaohongshu is the fastest-growing social commerce app in China, created for young women 18 to 35 years old, focused on fashion, beauty, and lifestyle. Founded in 2013, its name directly translates to "little red book", but it is known in English simply as RED. According to its own website, RED describes itself as a lifestyle sharing platform, although it can be thought of as Instagram meets Pinterest meets Amazon – a social, shoppable, video-led content platform fed with user-generated content. RED has earned a reputation for cultivating an experience known as "growing grass" (*zhongcao*)[60], a Chinese internet colloquialism referring to the FOMO (fear

---

60.   Zihao Liu, "Is Xiaohongshu Losing Steam?" *Jing Daily*, January 4, 2022. https://jingdaily.com/is-xiaohongshu-losing-steam/

of missing out) sensation of seeing a product owned by others and wanting it too. Growing grass has been lucrative. As of November 2021, RED was valued at US$20bn, with 300m registered users and 100m monthly active users[61]. For a frame of reference, this valuation puts RED at roughly the same size as Heineken beer or Toyota automotive globally[62].

The content on RED is a mix of captivating images that seem to spring from the pages of a fashion magazine as well as dynamic and addictive short-video content from users and brands alike – with frictionless integration from content to purchase, creating an irresistible shopping experience for users. The most lucrative format for generating sales has been livestreaming, which is part of what RED calls its "content to commerce"[63] system, which is an enabling innovation bundle that allows brands to directly connect and manage their marketing and selling relationships with consumers. Highly engaging and interactive, the livestreaming commerce feature leverages the closed loop from "online sharing" to "community interaction" which promotes brands and their products and builds a bridge to consumption – with high conversion, high repurchase rates, high customer orders, and low product return rates.[64] Global luxury brands such as Louis Vuitton, Givenchy, Gucci, and Tiffany find the Gen Z, affluent, female demographic of RED so compelling, they clamour for prime livestreaming slots.

---

61.   News Wire "China's Xiaohongshu raises $500 mln, valuation hits $20 bln", *Reuters*, November 8, 2021.

62.   Forbes Global 2000 List, *Forbes*, accessed July 23, 2022. https://www.forbes.com/lists/global2000

63.   Xiao Hong Shu Press Room, "Our New Content to Commerce System", September 10, 2021. https://www.xiaohongshu.com/en/newsroom/detail/empowering-small-businesses-with-our-new-content-to-commerce-system

64.   Xiao Hong Shu Press Room, "Our New Content to Commerce System".

How to Export This Catalyst

To Chinafy, businesses can scale by bridging and closing the gap between invention and impact with enabling, commercial innovations. The action of bridge building in the past in China often stemmed from necessity – typically related to a lack of the advanced economic and social conditions necessary for innovation to otherwise propagate. Yet these principles can be used to Chinafy anywhere in the world, to drive transformation in even the most sophisticated economies. With these principles there may never be an idea before its time, perhaps just ideas that need enabling innovations.

Map the Gaps

An innovator's goal is to reduce the lag time between invention and adoption, getting the innovation in use, by as many people as possible and as quickly as possible. Much can be gleaned from how Chinese innovators reduce lag time by identifying and tackling gaps, even turning potential stumbling blocks into levers for accelerated growth.

Often the bridges that need building are outside of the scope of the innovation. Some leaders might see these gaps as too big to tackle, "someone else's problem", or simply not part of the business's core capabilities. However, solving these gaps can be transformative for society and create sustained competitive advantage for the creator. So, while it might be tempting to see some barriers to adoption as outside the innovation's and innovator's remit, and therefore "not my problem", there are many compelling motivations for closing gaps and building bridges to shorten lag times and enable greater innovation impact.

To do so, first the business must have a good understanding of what gaps exist that could constrain or prevent adoption or growth. Start to scope these gaps by performing an audit of the ecosystem that surrounds the innovation and industry and map it to see the connections and linkages, identifying any social, regulatory, governmental, policy, community, activist, media, supplier, or environmental influencers. Once you have a view of the ecosystem, ask what actors, agencies, or policies might have a more substantial role to play than others in shaping the growth of the industry, or conversely constraining it? Are these actors currently facilitating the infrastructure or supporting conditions that would enable adoption or growth, or can they be influenced to do so? Or does your business need to explore gap-closing actions on enabling innovations independently to reduce lag time?

In the case of Alibaba, non-cash payment was a gap that had not been addressed by the banking industry and was clearly not a priority for development by the government or industry bodies. Had digital payment technology not been created outside the banking industry by Alibaba, it is unlikely e-commerce would have exploded in quite the same way or with the same speed as it did in China – the lag time could have easily been decades instead of years.

Whereas for social commerce in China, it was about creating a completely new, highly efficient content-to-commerce model that disrupted and improved the consumer journey by bolting on existing technologies to enable a new and dynamic business model. Unlike Alibaba and Alipay, there was no new invention, but mapping the ecosystem of available tools and technologies across both spheres of social and e-commerce enabled a recombination that ultimately yielded a new whole with far greater potential than the sum of its parts.

Launch in Beta

Also colloquially known as "launch and learn", launching in beta is about putting your product in the hands of a small group of users when it is 70–80% complete in order to get valuable learnings and make the necessary adjustments to perfect it for a broader release. Real users provide a valuable perspective and reality check on assumptions made in the creation and development process.

While launching in beta is typically an early attempt to test that you are solving your basic customer needs, to ensure your solution works as intended and to address any bugs in use, it can also be another way to identify and understand the gaps and barriers to adoption that might exist and create innovation scalability issues – potentially yielding new insight that may not have emerged during the ecosystem and gap mapping.

Leverage Both Market and Non-Market Strategies

With the ecosystem mapped and gaps or potential barriers to adoption identified, now it is time to ideate on the actions or enabling innovations that may be needed to build bridges to scale impact. These actions form the basis of your non-market strategy.

Chinese businesses recognize that non-market strategies are essential to generating more impactful outcomes. Rather than focusing solely on market strategy – the company's core activities in its current channels of trade with its suppliers and competitors – successful Chinese innovators layer both market and non-market strategies to build bridges for accelerated growth.

Chinese businesses have naturally become more adept at blending market and non-market strategies as historically, they faced a great many gaps in social and economic development. In the case of Alibaba, without tackling the payment issue with a digital shadow banking offer, neither Alibaba nor e-commerce would have flourished in China due to the lack of non-cash payment options to facilitate online transactions.

Yet, non-market strategies can be neglected elsewhere in the world as they are often seen outside of the fundamental remit of the business. However, Chinese businesses know that often this is the most fertile space for bridge-building to explode growth as it deeply considers the broader ecosystem in which the business or innovation lives. Industry development can be steered and influenced by identifying and tackling social, regulatory, governmental, policy, community, activist, media, supplier, and environmental barriers for growth. Further, when a business creates solutions that result in total value creation in society, these solutions generally pay back initially disproportionately to the creators, yielding a sustained competitive advantage[65].

To Chinafy, embrace the paradigm that companies are social and political entities and that a non-market strategy is equally important as a market strategy precisely because it has an important role to play in how industries, societies and economies develop. Areas to explore and questions to ask in creating a non-market strategy include:

- Can the regulatory environment be shaped or influenced? For example, if your product is in the drug space and is currently considered a prescription product, can you lobby or influence the regulatory environment to have it reclassified

---

65.   David Bach and David Bruce Allen, "What Every CEO Needs to Know About Non Market Strategy", *MIT Sloan Management Review Magazine*, Spring 2010 Edition.

as over-the-counter, enabling a simpler and faster route to market.

- Are there infrastructure or governmental gaps preventing adoption that can be closed with an enabling innovation? For example, if you are in the electric vehicle space and the lack of charging points is a barrier to purchase, can you build a bridge for the consumer by working with governments to adapt public parking spaces fit for purpose in key areas?
- If there are community concerns, can you overcome them? For instance, if your business is in the space of unmanned vehicles (cars or drones) and there are public safety concerns, can your business work with the community to find acceptable use cases or parameters?
- Can the media or even activists be of help in your mission? Imagine you are in plant-based food innovation, can you leverage topical health and wellness topics to generate a powerful case for behaviour change and generate discussion that is led by your business?

Chapter 5

Think Like a Futurist

CATALYST 3

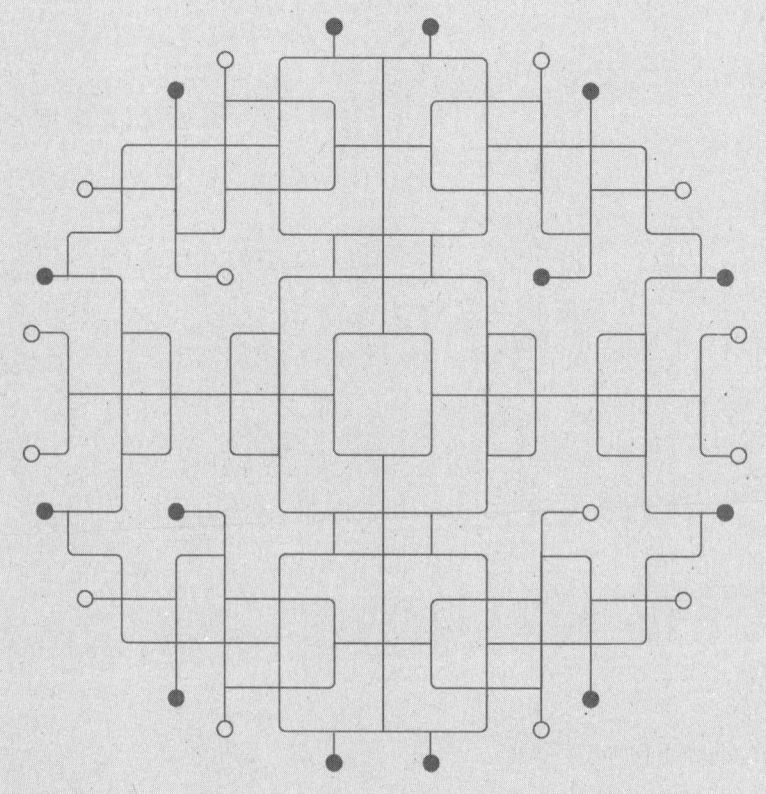

IF YOU ASKED SOMEONE in the late 19th century what would be desirable in personal transportation, they would likely have described a better horse and buggy; they wouldn't have said an automobile. This is because consumers not only struggle to articulate their unmet needs, but they also cannot imagine a new future, product, or service. They can only imagine the current realm of options and generally speculate on how to improve or modify existing offers.

This is because "demand is inchoate", asserts Paul Geroski in his book, *The Evolution of New Markets*. Geroski explains that unfortunately the demand of the market today is "not specific enough to give precise guidance to innovators."[66] The challenge is that for many new products and technologies, people don't yet know that they need or want them.

In today's world, we enthusiastically espouse the merits of listening to consumers and innovating off the basis of consumer feedback and user-centred design. While this is fertile ground for innovation, we must also acknowledge that the impact of visionary thinking cannot be underestimated. Outstanding visionaries from the West such as Elon Musk, Jeff Bezos and the late Steve Jobs have boldly imagined new futures for the world and society.

Yet, these visionaries are the exception. Most businesses rely on iterating and innovating their offer with existing or historical

---

66. Paul Geroski, *The Evolution of New Markets* (UK: Oxford University Press, 2003), p. 53.

information to make decisions as well as costly and time-consuming market research. A great many industries still spend hundreds of millions of dollars asking consumers what they want – in consumer products, 10% of annual sales revenue is allocated to acquiring market data and research. Unfortunately, wants are typically not the basis for new markets or disruptive value creation. This strategy leaves many businesses constantly chasing short-term gains, unable to do the long-range innovation they need to stay at minimum relevant and at best, ahead of the game.

Perhaps because market research, insight and data have historically been so fragmented, expensive, and unreliable in China, businesses never became dependent on looking to research to ask what the market wants. Further, after the re-opening of China to the world, in some ways it was necessary to navigate the way forward without looking backwards as there was little in the way of innovation in recent decades to draw from. This has forced Chinese society and businesses to think and behave as futurists no matter what industry they occupy, or the size of the business.

Instead of looking to historical blueprints for success, most Chinese businesses have needed to envision entirely new future states. What guides this thinking is dreaming big and focusing on solving problems for consumers and in society to innovate new realities as well as challenging the dominant design of any existing product or business model. This bold, visionary thinking is happening across industries in China, from the most mundane and everyday consumer products to complex, technology-driven businesses, and the ripple effect of this thinking will have global impact. These born-in-China unconventional approaches and business models can and do travel and will disrupt industries in the West.

Further to that, they are likely to be adopted by developing markets where China is making inroads with infrastructure, lending, and economic investments such as the continent of Africa, the developing countries in Southeast Asia of Vietnam, Cambodia and Laos, as well as developing nations in the Indian subcontinent such as Pakistan and Bangladesh. Imagine a future where these countries, so far behind today in development versus the EU and the US and the more prosperous countries in Asia such as Singapore and Korea, can potentially leapfrog the West with Chinese thinking and investment.

The Future of Drones

DJI, or Da Jiang Innovations, is a Shenzhen-based drone company founded in 2006 by then university student Frank Wang. The slogan, *Da jiang wu xian*, captures Wang's ambition, stating that DJI's dream and vision is so vast as to have no boundaries. Today, DJI is the world leader in drones, capturing over 70% of the market share of this US$40bn global industry in 2021; with a cumulative average growth rate of over 20%, this figure is expected to reach US$65bn by 2025.[67] It's an attractive industry with high growth potential and relatively low penetration, which has attracted many entrants who wish to capture this market potential. Yet none of the many entrants to drone manufacturing over the last 10–15 years across the US and EU have been able to catch up with DJI and many have gone out of business trying. So what has been the driving success behind DJI that makes it different?

---

67. Lucas Schrothi, "The Drone Market in 2021 and Beyond", *Drone Industry Insights,* August 10, 2021. https://droneii.com/the-drone-market-in-2021-and-beyond-5-key-takeaways

Like many tech businesses, DJI was started by students studying science and technology. Wang, originally from Zhejiang province, was attending the Hong Kong University of Science and Technology as an engineering graduate student when he decided to pursue his dream. As a child, he had always been fascinated with remote-controlled aircraft and model airplanes. At age 16, after receiving high marks on an exam, Wang was gifted a remote-controlled helicopter by his parents. The helicopter crashed on its first flight, leaving him disappointed as he waited for months for replacement parts to be shipped from Hong Kong.[68] As a young adult, he had a dream to create an aircraft that would accompany him on train rides and hikes, photographing his journey from above with a bird's-eye view. And most importantly, one that would not crash – the bane of remote-controlled aircraft enthusiasts at that time was the high crash rate of the devices, which made them unreliable in flight and potentially unsafe for bystanders.

Starting from his dorm room in Hong Kong and then eventually opening a small office in Shenzhen to be close to manufacturing for rapid prototyping, Wang and a couple of classmates began making drone components such as flight controllers and gimbals to supply drone manufacturers to fly more reliably. But the main goal was to ultimately launch DJI's own complete and affordable drone that was ready to fly straight out of the box for a mainstream hobbyist user such as Wang himself. Such a "tech toy" did not exist as yet. Most drones were expensive (over US$3000) and technical, requiring a degree of competency in assembly and flight. This meant that the average drone buyer was not an individual, but

---

68.   Ryan Mac, "Bow To Your Billionaire Drone Overlord: Frank Wang's Quest To Put DJI Robots Into The Sky", *Forbes*, May 6, 2015.

often organizations – usually police or military – using drones for surveillance.

Wang's dream was realized in 2013 with the Phantom 1 drone quad-copter launch. Costing US$700, The Phantom 1 was ready to fly straight out of the box, with a flight time of 10 minutes. While the device did not come equipped with a camera, an external camera could be mounted, though the resulting images and videos were a bit shaky. Later that year, the Phantom 2 with a flight time of 20 minutes, a range of 300 meters, and an integrated camera for high-quality HD photos and videos was launched. Still vulnerable to shakiness, further improvements were needed. In early 2014, the Phantom 2 Vision+, with a fully stabilized gimbal system, addressed this issue and further increased flight time to 25 minutes and range to 700 meters. Its stability and smoothness in flight enabled dynamic, creative images and video never before possible. As the most advanced, easy-to-use, affordable and reliable drone with remarkable image quality, the Phantom 2 Vision+ opened the door to a new vision for what drones could do and what purposes they could serve. In year 1, DJI's sales reached US$500m.[69] By 2015, this had doubled to US$1bn.[70]

In the US and Europe there was tremendous excitement over DJI's breakthroughs in drone technology. Companies like Amazon and DHL quickly focused on leveraging this technology for logistics and delivery and began testing the drones to see how they might be safely deployed. However, the risks for these kinds of applications, largely in urban areas, were high – many flight obstacles and

69.   Mac, "Bow To Your Billionaire Drone Overlord".
70.   Wai Fong Bah, Wee Kiat Lim, et al, "DJI Innovations: rise of the Drones", (Singapore: Nanyang Technical University, Nanyang Business School), September 19, 2017.

a high density of people meant that any failures, parcel drops, or crashes presented a real danger and could result in catastrophic human injury. This meant that aviation administrations now had an interest in regulating drone flight and that a licensing process for operators would be needed as well as a new category of liability and insurance to be created. The reality of achieving reliable drone delivery was going to be an exceedingly complex process, certainly one with a high return, but a long road of regulatory and safety issues to overcome.

Wang, however, had a different vision for this technology. In the history of technology, it is exceedingly rare that one company can gain a dominant market share as a product or device leaps from niche hobbyist to the mainstream – but this was Wang's vision. And Wang believed his vision would be realized by focusing more on reducing costs and providing models for different industries where flights were in less-populated areas and thus relatively free of risk. This led DJI into spaces such as construction for remote building checks, remote land surveys; video and film production for aerial photography and cinematography; agricultural applications for watering, crop dusting and surveillance; as well as disaster relief assessment and support. All of these were significantly more efficient and cost-effective than the current practices in these industries, which often rely on humans or expensive machinery and airplanes for these tasks. The commercial push of DJI was on top of the recreational and prosumer push where drone flight hobbyists were buying new models of DJIs drones as fast as they were released. Today there are drone races and closed-track racing courses and even a drone racing world championship. DJI has its own retail experience centres where consumers can not only purchase the drones and related equipment but also have an intimate experience with testing the latest model, seeing what upgrades or gadgetry can be added to enhance their experience, and also view experienced pilots flying drones in an enclosed wind tunnel. Part of DJI's success overseas in the hobbyist market as a "tech toy" was a strategic partnership with Apple to carry the product in its Apple stores – this meant that the first drone seen in the US and EU by Apple and tech enthusiasts was most likely a DJI.

While other competitors and industries continued to seek more complex logistics and military applications riddled with regulatory challenges, Wang was establishing market dominance anywhere and everywhere drones could be used, deftly navigating the spaces where drones could proliferate and wildly grow. To enhance the experience further, DJI focused on making the already user-friendly software easier and easier as well as reducing the price of the equipment. There's even a DJI platform, SkyPixel, for enthusiasts to share their photos and videos and engage with each other on tips. SkyPixel also hosts an annual photography competition with prizes totalling US₵100,000. Today, the Mavic range of DJI drones sell for as low as US$329, and some models are light enough not to require registration by aviation administrations as an aerial vehicle, can fly at a speed of 68.4 km/h (42.5 mph), enjoy 34-minute flight times, and can capture HDR imagery, including slow-motion video and panoramic photo and videos.

Wang's imagined future has been realized in only four years after launching his first drone as the first Chinese company to lead a global tech revolution. While DJI is a privately held company, analysts estimated its value at US$15bn in 2018.[71] In 2014, the world's

71. Medium, "How DJI Became the Drone Industry's Most Valued Company", January 4, 2019. https://medium.com/@askdroneu/

largest venture capital firm, Sequoia Capital, invested US$30m in DJI, whose valuation at that time was only US$1.6bn.[72] DJI's "future of drones" phenomenon is global – China accounts for only 20% of the total annual global sales. DJI's global sales come predominantly from outside China. North America, Europe and Asia (including China) each account for 30% share of sales, with the remaining 10% from South America and Africa.[73] While DJI is indeed facing some pressure from US and EU anti-China business sentiment and security concerns, it is still well-positioned to capture the exponential growth yet to come in Asia as well as South America and Africa. Predictions place the global drone market growth rate at 22% through to 2025[74], with the majority of that growth coming from developing economies where drones are a convenient and cost-effective tool for commercial applications in agriculture, infrastructure development and construction.

The Future of Tea

Annual sales of the tea market in China exceeded US$100bn in 2022; China is the world's largest tea market and still growing at 12.4%.[75]

how-dji-became-the-drone-industrys-most-valued-company-526f5bf6141d

72. Fangqi Xu and Hideki Muneyoshi, "A Case Study of DJI, the Top Drone Maker in the World", (Japan: Kindai University, Kindai Management Review), Volume 5, 2017.

73. Xu and Muneyoshi, "A Case Study of DJI".

74. Business Wire, "The Commercial Drones Global Market Report 2021", accessed May 11, 2022. https://www.businesswire.com/news/home/20210806005222/en/Commercial-Drones-Global-Market-Report-2021-Featuring-DJI-Parrot-SA-Aerovironmen-PrecisionHawk-and-Draganfly---ResearchAndMarkets.com

75. Statista, "Consumer Markets, Hot Tea", accessed May 13, 2022. https://www.statista.com/outlook/cmo/hot-drinks/tea/china

To put this in perspective, this is 2x larger than the sugar industry in the US[76]; and to compare it on a business level, tea in China is an industry larger than Facebook (Meta Group) but slightly smaller than General Motors in the 2021 Fortune 500 Ranking.

In China, tea is in the fibre of culture. While businesses like Starbucks have brought coffee to China and introduced at least two generations of Chinese to coffee beverages and coffee culture, tea continues to dominate daily life. Considering that China has undergone a great deal of change in the last 30 years, tea remains one of the comforting and familiar things that is deeply rooted and historically unchanging in Chinese culture.

That is until Hey Tea was launched in China in 2012. Hey Tea was a single location for three years until their expansion in 2015. Now they total 650 outlets in China selling what can only be described as the future of tea for China. Hey Tea has evolved tea drinking from a daily ritual at home and in traditional Chinese tea houses to a modern, lifestyle brand that potentially has more in common with a fashion brand than a food or beverage brand. Routinely queues can be seen outside of Hey Tea's locations, usually in upscale shopping areas, with customers lining up and snapping selfies while waiting up to 6 hours to order and drink their teas.

The locations themselves are futuristic, minimalist, decorated in white with natural blond wood and often with limited dine-in seating as many orders are takeaway. The logo is prominent in-store and on packaging and features a hand-drawn cartoon illustration of a man drinking tea from a large cup, as opposed to the small thimble-sized cups used to drink tea in the traditional manner.

76.   Statista, "Agriculture", accessed May 13, 2022. https://www.statista.com/
      statistics/1283819/global-sugar-manufacturing-market-value/

The brand name features the words "Hey Tea" with much more prominence than the Chinese characters, suggesting an international perspective. Yet, the product range is highly innovative and original, created in China for China. The best-selling product is their Cheezo Tea – a drink of flavoured cold tea with a frothy layer of whipped cream cheese on top – which can be served in salty or sweet versions. Their bubble tea with tapioca pearls and fruit teas are also popular. Hey Tea's offerings are all premium, selling for RMB25–35 (US$3.50–$5.00) – a 3–4x markup from other ready-to-drink tea options, and a 2x markup versus other premium, modern tea cafes.

With distinctive packaging that is highly recognizable, featuring a transparent cup so that the vibrant tea colours are highly visible and provide a striking backdrop for the logo, taking an afternoon stroll with a cup of Hey Tea has badge value that is social currency on social media in China. In fact, Hey Tea is known as a *wanghong* brand – "wanghong" means internet celebrity in Chinese. Wanghong brands are those that build their brand following and engagement by publishing stylish photos, videos, and other content online for their fans – a practice more common among pricey sports and fashion brands than tea shops. Hey Tea further gamifies the social experience by running a scavenger hunt competition to find new product releases in store- or city-based limited editions.

Hey Tea is also famous for its frequent co-branding campaigns, which reach all aspects of their trendy consumer's lifestyle – from fashion-driven makeup and clothing to entertainment-driven stereos, electronics and mahjong sets. Hey Tea even has a range of condoms. City-level products and merchandising have an irresistible draw for local consumers and have featured co-branding with W Hotel in Guangzhou as well as Beijing-branded items in the country's capital. While these collectibles are no doubt inspired by the Starbucks playbook of city mugs, items such as reusable shopping bags, umbrellas and phone cases are more suitable for younger consumers and also are importantly for use out-of-home, which have the impact of further promoting the brand.

Hey Tea has also addressed the issue of queues and wait times with its Hey Tea Go app which allows for easy pre-order, pick-up, and cashless digital payments. The app, which has solved the convenience issue, is also cleverly linked to social media, where consumers can "announce" to their followers they are at Hey Tea or drinking Hey Tea. Within six months of the app's launch in 2017, it reached 4m users, with a repurchase rate of 300%, and daily active users reaching 170,000.[77] As of 2020, the Hey Tea Go app reported having 10m users, who generate over half of sales.[78]

The app further evolved to have paid membership programmes starting at RMB179 (approximately US$26) per year. Members receive high-value coupons and vouchers that encourage more purchases and generously exceed the annual fee. Every aspect of the user experience is gamified, with new levels of membership being unlocked with greater spending, giving members privileges such as VIP fast passes, buy-one-get-one-free vouchers, double-points credits, and even birthday gifts.

Hey Tea's digital engagement and purchasing is not only important for a modern consumer demanding a frictionless lifestyle, but

---

77. Caroline Lai, "On Creating Tea Culture 2.0", ChinaTech Blog, November 23, 2020. https://www.chinatechblog.org/blog/heytea-on-creating-tea-culture-2-0-2-2

78. Grace Ong, "Bubble Tea Brand Hey Tea Launches Mobile App Sees Repurchase Rate Triple", Marketing Interactive, February 3, 2020. https://www.marketing-interactive.com/bubble-tea-brand-heytea-launches-mobile-app-sees-purchase-rate-triple

it also is an essential tool for understanding the consumers from a product development point of view. Consumers easily tire of the same old flavours and are eager to try new products. The app yields an incredible amount of data and insight that allows Hey Tea to create new, exciting offers and leverage co-branding with agility, shortening product development from a typical six-month time frame to a mere three months, thereby giving consumers almost endless variety, as well as making the product and brand experience joyful and increasingly sticky.

During the pandemic, Hey Tea modified their offer to add contactless delivery, installing lockers that could be activated with a code for consumers to pick up their drinks. To compensate for the lack of physical experience in Hey Tea cafes, Hey Tea increased its activity on Chinese social media platform Douyin (TikTok) to drive daily active users, launching the "Draw Your Hey Tea" hashtag campaign. One single post reached 1.7m likes, and the hashtag became the most popular on the platform.[79] It's this continuous innovation, an original approach to product and flavour innovation, a brand experience which is more like that of a lifestyle brand than a quick service cafe, and a gamified app that is driving the future of tea in China.

In China, the highest-grossing stores sell an average of 3,000 cups of tea a day, yielding daily returns of RMB100,000 (approximately US$15,000).[80] In June 2021, Hey Tea was valued at US$9.27bn, and has high-powered venture capital investors such as Tencent and Sequoia Capital China.[81] For comparison, Hey Tea's val-

---

79.   Lai, "On Creating Tea Culture 2.0".
80.   Lai, "On Creating Tea Culture 2.0".
81.   PanDaily, "Hey Tea to Complete New Round of Funding for a 9.47 Billion", June 25, 2021. https://pandaily.com/

uation is larger than American chain Dunkin' Donuts, which operates over 14,000 locations in 42 countries.[82] Hey Tea has recently expanded beyond mainland China to Hong Kong and now opened overseas in Singapore and Malaysia.

The Future of Social Influencers

All over the world, KOLs, or key opinion leaders, are becoming the backbone of marketing for many brands and businesses. KOLs are people who are considered experts or influential thought leaders on topics ranging from fashion, cooking, health and wellness to more serious spaces such as investing, business transformation and innovation. These are people who generally have the power to move markets, leveraging their enormous social media followings. As a result of their power and influence, some charge as much as US$500,000 per post, like Kim Kardashian in the US who enjoys 177m followers. In China, one famous influencer, Austin Li Jiaqi, known as the "Lipstick King", sold US$1.7bn of cosmetics in 12 hours of livestreaming on Alibaba during China's famous 11/11 Singles Day sale, garnering 250m views.[83] Another top KOL, Viya, sold US$1.25bn worth of products in her 14-hour livestream marathon in the same selling period.[84] While these KOLs can generate massive sales, they also come at a high cost – after all you get what you pay for, and China

heytea-to-complete-new-round-of-funding-for-9-27-billion/
82. Companies Market Cap, May 2022. https://companiesmarketcap.com/dunkin-brands/marketcap/#:~:text=Market%20cap%3A%20%248.77%20Billion,market%20cap%20of%20%248.77%20Billion
83. Huileng Tan, "China Lipstick King Sold 1.7 Billion in Stuff in 12 Hours", *Business Insider*, October, 22, 2021. https://www.businessinsider.com/china-lipstick-king-sold-17-billion-stuff-in-12-hours-2021-10
84. Tan, "China Lipstick King".

KOL fees are generally not so different from the six-figure fees of top Hollywood stars.

There's obviously the downside of KOLs as well – they are human after all. Cancel culture is real globally, and nowhere more so than China, where even the government takes an active role. In March 2022, Chinese heartthrob and celebrity actor Deng Lun's social media accounts, with followers totalling 60m, were scrubbed by Chinese authorities when Deng was found to be guilty of tax evasion and fined RMB106m (US$16.7m).[85] International companies like Unilever and L'Oréal, as well as local companies like appliance maker Viomi and dairy company Junlebao, immediately dropped contracts with the film, TV and Netflix actor upon learning that Deng had been accused of hiding personal income earnings in fake business deals. In fact, the aforementioned KOL livestreamer Viya was fined RMB1.34bn (US$210m) for tax evasion in 2021.[86] These are just two examples in a slew of many celebs who have been cancelled due to scandals, allegations of rape and even non-illegal behaviour deemed to not be in line with Chinese cultural norms.

It is for this reason and many others that China is innovating with virtual KOLs. Imagine an influencer who is highly aspirational, represents the ideal beauty and image standards, and whose persona can be curated by brands or marketing agencies. Thanks to advanced animation and AI, virtual influencers are visually indistinguishable

85. Mandy Zuo, "Chines Heartthrob Deng Lun's Career in Limbo", South China Morning Post, March 16, 2022. https://www.scmp.com/news/people-culture/china-personalities/article/3170685/chinese-heartthrob-deng-luns-career-limbo

86. Reuters, "China Tells Celebrities, Livestreamers to Report Tax Related Crimes by 2022", NBC News, December 22, 2021. https://www.nbcnews.com/news/world/china-tells-celebrities-livestreamers-report-tax-related-crimes-2022-rcna9616

from humans, but unlike humans, they never age, gain weight, have a scandal, or say or do anything undesirable for a brand. Further to that, aside from the cost of creation, they do not have exorbitant fees or talent residual payments, they can work 24 hours a day, do not need breaks and can appear in many places at one time. These virtual idols always have perfect skin, a ready smile, a twinkle in the eye and are fast on their way to becoming a billion-dollar industry. Another big advantage is the ability of virtual KOLs to interact with and collect data from every single consumer – a data goldmine for brands and businesses.

It is not only the cost savings, data collection potential and flawless perfection of these virtual celebrities that appeal to both brands and consumers; it is also what it says about a brand that uses them, placing them in a forward-thinking, tech-savvy realm, even if they are simply selling something as basic as ice-cream. And while it might seem that perfection is not all that relatable, Chinese consumers report this is part of a virtual idol's appeal. When a female consumer in her 30s was interviewed about the appeal of her favourite virtual influencer Ling, she reported that Ling's AI perfection made her "effortlessly cool" and a "moving art piece", and because Ling was so flawless, she did not compare herself to Ling in the same way she would to a real celebrity.[87]

The bottleneck of the content-hungry world of social media is no longer constrained by KOL or celeb casting, shooting, and editing. Now highly curated, custom content with compelling, aspirational virtual KOLs can be generated 24 hours a day. It is no surprise then

---

87. Cheryl Teh, "China is Tempting Customers with Its Flawless AI Influencers", Insider, August 13, 2021. https://www.insider.com/chinas-flawless-ai-influencers-the-hot-new-queens-of-advertising-2021-8

that it is estimated that the virtual influencer business in China is worth US$960m and experiencing 70% year-on-year growth.[88]

How to Export This Catalyst

No matter the industry – whether in the space of high tech or everyday consumer staple goods – futurist thinking can be applied to Chinafy the business and catalyse exponential growth.

Challenge the Dominant Design

Every industry, no matter how established, can be ripe for disruption. A key principle of disruption is challenging the dominant design. The dominant design is the form or design an industry has adopted as the industry standard – for example, cars have four wheels, or the internet relies on a hardwired cable, MBA education must always be in the classroom, or spirits must always have alcohol. These are all examples of dominant design that have been disrupted.

In the case of Hey Tea in China, the dominant design for tea was tea served hot and unadulterated and typically consumed at home or in traditional tea houses. While there were fanciful tea options already available, like inexpensive bubble tea, which were popular with the younger generations, Hey Tea's model imagined the future of tea to be one of experiential indulgence, blending the worlds of beverages, gourmet snacks and desserts, and activating this new world with digital transformation, chic retail outlets, and iconic branding with strong badge value, becoming a social status symbol when seen in the hands of consumers. Meanwhile, DJI challenged the dominant design of drone flight, which was predicated

---

88.   Teh, "China is Tempting Customers with Its Flawless AI Influencers".

on complex equipment, requiring expert assembly, and operated by experienced pilots, versus the DJI vision for the future, which was a simplified UAV (unmanned aerial vehicle) which could be a tech toy and operated by anyone, straight out of the box. With regard to KOLs, the dominant design was aspirational celebrities with strong social media followings, which was reimagined to be about virtual idols who build social media followings on the basis of carefully cultivated personas and curated content.

What assumptions do you or your industry hold to be immutable? Do you know for sure that these cannot be modified, improved, or shifted along an existing or possibly even a new performance continuum? The key to redefining the dominant design is to find and challenge core assumptions and seek ways to transform the existing industry with new trajectories of performance, thereby opening new opportunities for innovation. This is the path of new value creation as opposed to incremental innovation that improves the existing offer in the short term along its existing vectors of performance.

To Chinafy, the process of iteratively disrupting the dominant design is highly valued not only for speed of development but also because the experimentation and learning from the end user are valuable in creating a new shape of things. Failures and missteps along the way provide important information about what can and cannot be changed or challenged in the dominant design. It is impossible to perfectly predict the future and thus a futurist must be open to recognizing when they have placed the wrong bets and avoid being slavish to the vision or developing tunnel vision such that they ignore and fail to acknowledge relevant, challenging inputs and information. What is more important than failure is how a business responds and how learnings are successfully mined to refine and define the path to a new future. In fact, in China failure is largely destigmatized in business as it is viewed as an opportunity to give a business more practice in adapting to change, shifting to respond to new information as well as honing the organization's ability to shape and shift long-term thinking.

Employ Three Sights: Insight, Cross-sight, Foresight

As Geroski stated, demand is inchoate. Demand can be thought of as consumer needs and wants, which can only be shaped by current experiences and expectations with existing offers. As such, counter-intuitive to how many businesses behave, consumer demand in fact plays a small role in defining new futures. However, new futures can be imagined, and opportunities unlocked by using the Three Sights model: insight, cross-sight and foresight.

Insight is about looking to known factors, such as the market and users, but with a view to excavating new white spaces and gaps. It is a completely different orientation from the traditional model of user insight which focuses on directly speaking to consumers about how they would suggest improving existing products. For the futur-ist, gathering insight looks more like taking a step back to gain a bird's-eye view of unmet needs, pain points for which there are no current solutions, or even gaps in broader lifestyle ambitions which are not yet realized. For example, globally, "frictionless living" is a consumer lifestyle ambition that has inspired many successful apps, services, gadgets, and devices. Many offers have been improved by using "frictionless living" as a guiding principle – for example, DJI making a drone that is ready to fly out of the box, or Hey Tea facili-tating frictionless purchasing and consumption with their app.

Cross-sight suggests you look outside your world and industry to examine related worlds. To Chinafy, this might mean explor-ing completely different industries or adjacent categories to seek relevant parallel insights. Some say that DJI took a page out of the Apple playbook setting up their own retail stores which allowed potential buyers to interact with the product, demo the drones and speak to the sales staff which were experienced users themselves. Could it be that Hey Tea looked to what Starbucks had done for coffee, innovating coffee with offerings like the Frappuccino and Pumpkin Spiced Latte, and asked themselves if the same could be done for tea? In the space of virtual KOLs, might the entertainment industry have looked at what was happening in AI technology and imagined how that might be applied within their industry?

The third sight is foresight, which is about imagining where the industry could be in 5–10 years. This is the space of true visioning, and to Chinafy with foresight is to create entirely new realities for how people might live, play, or work. As a starting point, it is important to look at the global or macro societal trends that hold influence and are likely to have influence for the next decade or more. A macro trend is something that is big and broad, for example environmentalism, and can be observed across multiple industries. There may be several manifestations of this macro trend across food, transport, energy, travel and more. As foresight is simply a plausible view of the future, you can mine the macro trends to design the next decade for your brand and business. For example, assuming environmentalism continues strongly as a macro trend, how might this take shape in your industry, what trajectories in your business might emerge from a zero-waste, carbon-neutral, traceable supply chain future? If you are an ice-cream business, this might look a lot like cultivating the exploration of new ingredients and moving more to plant-based products, given dairy farming's impact on the environment. Or perhaps you need to reinvent the product such that it can be shelf-stable, not requiring a cold supply chain, and frozen only before use. Perhaps it means reimagining a refill system that relies on multiple-use containers. These are not unimaginable futures, but instead very real trajectories in an industry that might determine whether your business is still around in 5–10 years. To Chinafy by anticipating the future enables industries to capture this value first and become the architects of explosive growth and transformation.

Of course, external factors can also bring sudden change. While your business might be in a high-growth industry today, it does not mean that this business growth will continue unfettered – even if the industry continues to grow. For example, in the case of DJI, while the demand is very much still present for simple and affordable drone flight, there have been increasing security concerns leading US and EU companies to cancel contracts with DJI, worried that the data collected by the drones can be accessed by the Chinese government. For DJI, this has hindered their growth trajectory in 2022, so they must pivot in terms of new growth opportunities. For DJI, likely the next realm of development will be looking to markets that have good relationships with China, or even looking to innovate on data collection and storage to be able to ensure unequivocally that their users' data is private. Pivoting when facing external influences that shift the three sights is critical for long-term survival.

Dream Big

Dreaming big and having a future vision allows you to see patterns you might not ordinarily spot – which then enables you to see the path forming as you are on it. This is often referred to in China as "building the car as you are driving it", a colloquial expression that embodies the notion of the action of forward motion itself having the enabling potential to help you to identify the path ahead. Much like when driving at night, you have a destination in mind, but the head lamps only allow you to see some short measure ahead – but if you have the destination in mind, you can trust that this short view will help you navigate the road to the destination.

This sort of dreaming-big navigation involves taking the perspective of two views. The Institute for the Future describes this as the Two Curve Framework[89] and asserts that at any given moment, we are living on two curves. The curve we are on is "today's way of doing things" and is on a downward trajectory. Simultaneously, we are also on another curve which is emerging and on an upward trajectory, and this curve can be thought of as "tomorrow's way of doing things". The challenge is we do not know the rate of decline or emergence, but if we keep an eye out for signals, we can often identify the path more clearly. The point at which these two curves meet is where big dreams can shift into reality and where transformation takes place.

It's important also to consider that these curves might be from two seemingly unrelated areas. In the case of virtual KOLs, the diminishing curve represented the challenges of celebrity and spokespeople influence. In China, with celebrities meeting society and government cancel culture as well as becoming increasingly unaffordable with rising fees, a disturbing volatility in the KOL industry emerged. This downward curve met the rising curve of animation and AI technology, leading to an open door for production and animation companies to reshape KOL culture and the celebrity spokesperson economy.

---

89. Marina Gorbis, "Five Principles for Thinking Like a Futurist", *Educause Review*, March 11, 2019. https://er.educause.edu/articles/2019/3/five-principles-for-thinking-like-a-futurist

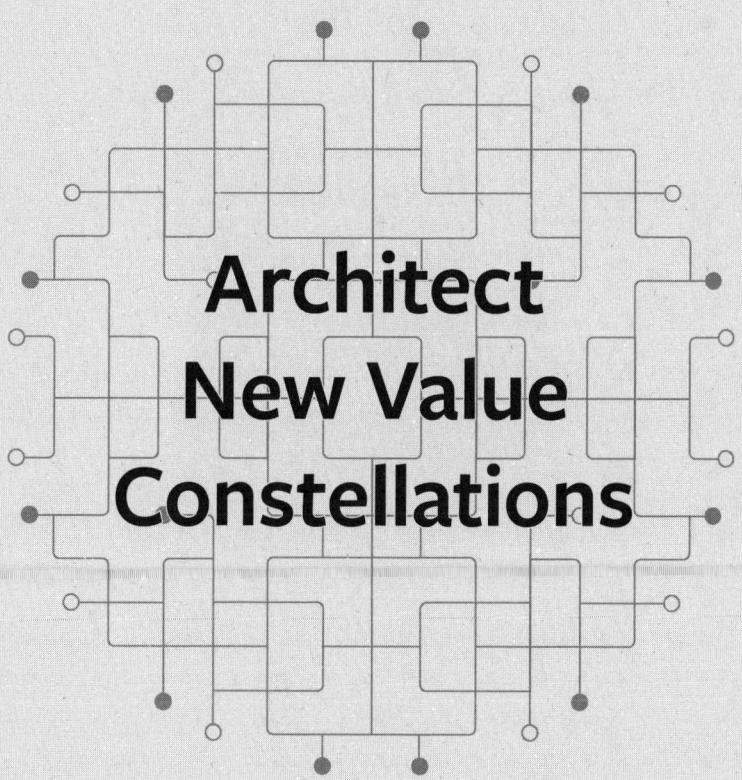

Chapter 6

Architect New Value Constellations

CATALYST 4

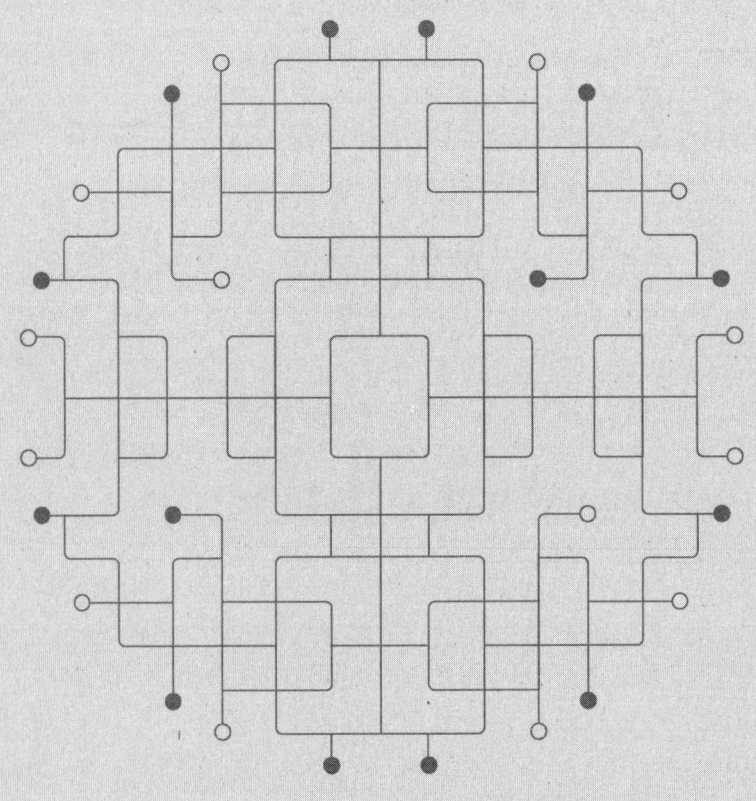

IF YOU ARE FROM a Western culture and have ever attended a business meeting in China, it may have been a frustrating experience. Business meetings in China serve a different purpose from what you might be used to. In Western culture, meetings are designed to be an efficient, goal-oriented gathering of key decision-makers to drive alignment and decision-making. In China, meetings are ritualized gatherings for building relationships whose main goal is to deepen mutual understanding. In Chinese business meetings, many people from all levels of an organization attend as a delegation, pleasantries and gifts are exchanged at length, and each side presents their views in full without interruption. There are generally no open disagreements or debates if the viewpoints differ, and there would be no meaningful attempts to resolve differences in this forum. In fact, it is exceedingly rare to arrive at an outright commitment or decision in a meeting. This often leaves the Western visitors wondering what the point of the meeting was at all! However, this type of interaction stems from Asian cultural biases which not only shape meetings, but also shape how innovation and businesses form and grow in China.

In studies that consider the impact of culture on how people see and interpret the world, it is observed that in Asia thinking is more context-based; whereas in the West, thinking is more object-based.[90]

---

90. Bruce Bower, "Cultures of Reason: Thinking Styles May Take Eastern and Western Routes", *Science News* 157.4 January 22, 2000, pp. 56–58.

What this means is in Asia, people see things as interconnected and seek to understand the relationships between them and their interdependence and interactions. In the West, people tend to focus more on the object and analyze the details of that object, grouping objects or traits into similar categories using formal logic or rules.

This cultural thinking bias significantly impacts the approach to innovation. In the West, managers might focus on getting product features and details 100% right, whereas in Asia, managers might focus on getting the external partners or collaborations in place to make the product a success. Both are important, but it's the focus of each perspective that leads to very different activities, and often with very different outcomes.

Chinese businesses have always actively sought to broaden their reach through the network effect of vertical integration, partnerships and collaboration. In fact, this notion can be understood in the Chinese concept of *guanxi*. In China, guanxi is the personal network structure and connections that enable things to get done, open doors and close deals. It is a concept that generally applies to personal networking but given it is so ingrained in the local culture, we can think of it as a cultural concept and orientation that has broader influence on how people build and conduct business. Individuals and businesses see the broader context and interdependencies and actively seek to identify and obtain the support and connections needed to make things happen. Naturally this concept and way of seeing relationships also extends to innovation. In innovation this manifests as the architecture of meaningful value "constellations".

Possibly the most tangible evidence of this can be found in China's sprawling digital platforms and super apps, e.g., Tencent's WeChat. The success of these digital platforms is often viewed from the lens of Western bias as a result of China's great firewall and the blocking of the Western alternatives of Facebook, eBay, Instagram, Google, YouTube and more. However, this is a myopic view with a limited understanding of the unique ecosystems these offers have created by architecting completely new and powerful value constellations.

Consider the vast Alibaba ecosystem – it is often compared to Amazon plus eBay plus PayPal plus Apple Pay plus Google plus individual retailer websites. In fact, Alibaba Group is a completely vertically integrated value constellation of anything and everything related to online shopping and search, as well as the customer support needed to make this happen across all potential audiences of B2B, B2C and C2C – including digital payments, financing, logistics, cloud computing and data management, and e-commerce advertising and marketing support. This blended ecosystem puts together the services needed for maximum utility and convenience to support buyers and sellers. A key difference with Alibaba versus Amazon is that Alibaba does not compete with their sellers with own-label products. They are brand partners, generating an unparalleled value constellation for their customers. Notably, Alibaba helps brands succeed by sharing data and recommendations on how to more effectively present and sell products – thus providing true partnership value and creating brand preference over other e-commerce channels. Alibaba, while the biggest at 51% market share of the China e-commerce universe,[91] is not the only game in town, with strong competitors in the form of JD.com and Pinduoduo. These

---

91. Dashveenjit Kaur, "Alibaba Risks Dominance in China as Shoppers Evolve", techwireasia.com, November 9, 2021. https://techwireasia.com/2021/11/alibaba-risks-dominance-in-china-as-shoppers-evolve/

competitors, however, provide less sales and purchase support. In other words, Alibaba's competitors have weaker value constellations.

Alibaba is the classic China example, but let's look at a newer player – ByteDance's Douyin, or TikTok as it is known outside of China. Douyin is new breed of digital ecosystem – a social media, video entertainment platform with a shopping cart. Almost every item in Douyin's 15-second videos is for sale and can be bought directly on the site or app. One wonders why this is not the case with YouTube? Douyin's unique vision for social commerce has led to an online selling innovation – livestreaming sales, similar to a television-style infomercial format. Livestreaming sales leverage the full social power of the platform: there is a group-buy option with friends for discounts; live commenting and questions form a social hub for the presenter and audience to engage together; purchases can be posted as personal recommendations or links shared to join in the livestreaming sale audience. When Douyin launched, knowing most users in China engage with social media on smartphones over cellular data networks (WiFi is not commonly available outside of first- and second-tier cities), ByteDance put together Douyin-branded cellular data packages with local mobile providers, thus architecting a powerful value constellation between app and mobile data that enabled rapid scaling. These packages offered 25% of the normal data price to use Douyin services.[92] Thus, in effect, Douyin subsidized its own growth by lowering the cost for users – an investment they will easily recover by monetizing the channel and becoming the leader in livestreaming sales.

92.   Deng Feng, Professor, Digital Marketing, NYU Shanghai. *Interview, NYU Shanghai campus*, November 20, 2019.

WeChat: Arguably the Most Powerful Value Constellation in the World

WeChat, or Weixin as it is known in China, has evolved from its start in 2011 as an instant messaging app to a service that has become known as the "operating system" of China, meeting the daily needs of over 1.27bn monthly active users (as of Q4 2021)[93] across China and more broadly, Asia. This makes WeChat one of the most successful software products in history and has catapulted its parent company Tencent into one of the top 10 companies in the world by market capitalization[94] alongside tech giants such as Apple, Microsoft and global behemoths like Saudi Aramco oil company and Visa credit services.

How did an instant messaging app become arguably the world's most powerful value constellation of services? Over 10 years, WeChat consistently innovated to add more features, functionality and cross-pollination with other apps and services such that it has become a portal to all features of daily life. On WeChat, you can instant message, search the internet, share photos or documents, send or receive payment to vendors or individuals, book a taxi or ride-share car service, book a flight, train or hotel, manage the payment of your utilities and mobile phone, apply for a loan or manage your wealth portfolio, donate to charity, access your medical records, shop from any of your favourite brands, book gym classes and manage membership, stream videos, order food delivery, buy

93. China Internet Watch Report, "WeChat Users and Platform Insights 2022", May 18, 2022. https://www.chinainternetwatch.com/31608/wechat-statistics/
94. Julian Birkinshaw, Dickie Liang-Hong Ke, Enrique de Diego, "Innovation and Agility at Tencent's WeChat", Case Study, London Business School, August 2019.

movie, concert or sports tickets, conduct group-buys, sell or buy used goods, find housing to buy or rent... the list is seemingly endless. A whole book in and of itself could be written about WeChat and its functionality, but more important than what WeChat enables users to do is how it architected such a meaningful value constellation for users such that life without WeChat is unimaginable to those who use it. The app is so transformative that when many Chinese travel to countries where WeChat is less penetrated, they feel as if they have stepped 10 years back in time.

Initially in 2011, with WeChat offering only the free text messaging function, the three big mobile phone operators joined up to collectively oppose the app and lodged complaints with government oversight agencies, seeing WeChat as a free SMS service and therefore a threat to their existing large revenues from SMS services. To convert mobile providers into allies, WeChat partnered with China Unicom, one of the big three providers, developing a data card pilot programme to demonstrate how mobile providers could make even more revenue from data charges than SMS fees.

In the first stage of development, frequent releases surprised users with new functionality such as group chat and voice messaging. However, WeChat was not growing rapidly as there were several local competitors – for example, the dominant internet chat provider QQ had recently launched a mobile version. However, it was with voice messaging that the app really took off as voice messaging was new and different and represented real communication with intonation and emotion for users – something that people were eager to try. Mobile phones did not have voicemail functionality and answering machines were not the norm in China, where many homes did not have land lines and had already leapfrogged to mobile. Voice and video calling soon followed. Another breakthrough innovation for users was Moments, a social feed where users could post photos and videos visible to those in their contact list – this further differentiated it from other chat-only providers and even had functionality that differentiated it from social apps which were based on text posts with photos being rarely posted. Also, unlike other social media, pictures, likes or comments could not be seen by friends of friends, so there was more of a feeling of a closed social group with privacy, with WeChat seeking to "create a tool that belonged to the mobile network from the inside out".[95] Later, a new and unique function, People Nearby, enabled users to find people and make new friends by shaking their phone, which would signal to users who also had People Nearby open and who were in a certain radius that they were open to connect and chat. This first stage of development created an incredibly useful communication and social platform that amassed 100m users in 433 days.[96]

In the second stage of development, digital payments and a Services section of the app were added. A bank account could be linked to the profile and through the new WeChat Pay offer, users could send payments to a variety of institutions as well as individuals. The new Services functionality allowed WeChat to actively bring in third parties such as ride hailing apps, utility companies, travel websites and more as partners with operations in the platform. Buttons were added which allowed users to click to access utility companies and their bills to view and pay them. All hardcopy bills sent by mail featured a QR code that could be scanned to pay and prompted users upon doing so to link to their WeChat for future

---

95.   Birkinshaw et al., "Innovation and Agility at Tencent's WeChat".
96.   Birkinshaw et al., "Innovation and Agility at Tencent's WeChat".

convenience. There were buttons to book travel via a third-party provider that consumers were already familiar with, with special pricing for WeChat users. Users could click a transportation button to order a taxi or hail a ride-sharing car, also using existing providers. In restaurants or shops, users could scan QR codes to conveniently pay, without the need for cash exchange. Money could be sent to friends and contacts in the chat function of the app, enabling easy bill sharing. However as digital payments were still nascent, WeChat decided to implement a novel play to give users a reason to send money digitally with a "hongbao" feature. This was a playful digital take on the practice of giving hongbao, or red envelopes, with cash gifts – a practice that is customary over Chinese New Year, but also a common way of saying thank you in Chinese culture. As intended, this kickstarted the use of WeChat Pay and helped it rapidly close the gap with competitor Alipay, who had launched more than a year earlier.

By integrating payment to many providers through the Services section of the app, WeChat began to become a convenience hub for users, serving as a booking, planning and payment portal for frictionless living. The market-leading ride-hailing app DiDi (the Uber of China) operates within WeChat and reported that the majority of DiDi users access the service through WeChat and not through the DiDi app. China Telecom reported most monthly mobile bills or pay-as-you-go SIM top-ups were paid within WeChat and not through their own payment channels. Initially WeChat had a plan to charge third parties an ongoing rate for these services but decided to make it free with only a RMB300 (approximately US$48 in 2013) certification fee to verify the identity of the party. Gerald Hu, Head of Business, WeChat Open Platforms, recalled, "They said we were 'buddha-like' in that we were helping others... but we saw it like honeybees that will benefit from the honey that pollinates the flowers."[97]

In the next stage, Official Accounts were created that enabled brands and businesses to have direct contact with their consumers in WeChat, communicating directly to consumers about their brands, products and services. By the end of 2014, there were 8m Official Accounts on WeChat.[98] It was an easy place for consumers to see a fitness centre schedule or be notified that their favourite clothing shop was running a seasonal promotion. By the end of 2016, with all these innovations and the high-functioning ecosystem of utility for users, WeChat's monthly active users exploded to close to 900m,[99] an astounding five-year growth trajectory that was unparalleled in the history of apps anywhere in the world. By 2016, WeChat was also present outside of China, used in Southeast Asia, India and Latin America, as well as many places where Chinese residents or tourists could be found. WeChat scan codes for payment were as likely to be found in name-brand luxury stores in New York City or London as they were in Shanghai or Guangzhou.

In 2017, in the third stage of development, WeChat launched Mini-Programs. Mini-Programs were sub-applications, or an app within an app, for businesses to run directly in the WeChat app, with WeChat Pay frictionlessly linked. On Mini-Programs, groceries can be ordered from Aldi or pizza from Pizza Hut; clothing from Lululemon or Zara; makeup and toiletries from Sephora or Watsons; fitness classes or doctor's appointments can be booked and more.

---

97.   Birkinshaw et al., "Innovation and Agility at Tencent's WeChat".
98.   Birkinshaw et al., "Innovation and Agility at Tencent's WeChat".
99.   Tingyi Chen, "The Top 500 WeChat Official Accounts", Walk the Chat Trend Report, June 11, 2017. https://walkthechat.com/trend-report-top-500-wechat-official-account/

What is particularly interesting about WeChat Mini-Programs is how small businesses and entrepreneurs leveraged this function as a turnkey e-commerce solution. Mini-Programs had great utility for these businesses, cutting out the need for distributors and giving them a direct-to-consumer channel for not only sales, but also a platform where they could engage consumers in chat, provide customer service, distribute advertising and other service messages – making a business's Mini-Program a fully functioning selling and communications channel. Mini-Programs were easier to build and could be created for about 20% of the cost of a standalone app.[100] Furthermore, they didn't require users to download, install or register – all the necessary information could be carried over from WeChat, and payment was enabled by WeChat Pay. Users could just use the Mini-Program and leave it without yet another app cluttering their phone.

Allen Zhang, WeChat creator and chief developer, spoke about the power of the platform in 2019: "WeChat's driving force can be summarized in two points... First, to create a good tool that can keep up with the times... The second driving force is to let creators cultivate value. After the Official Accounts Platform got started, WeChat began to reflect the advantages of being a platform, later including Mini-Programs. When a platform only focuses on pursuing its own benefits, it won't last. When a platform creates benefits for others, it takes on a life of its own.... A lot of people do not understand why Mini-Programs are decentralized. If we didn't decentralize it, Tencent could monopolize the platform with its own Mini-Programs and there would be no external developers. Sure, Tencent would benefit in the short term, but the platform ecosystem would not."

---

100. Birkinshaw et al., "Innovation and Agility at Tencent's WeChat".

It is estimated that by building a powerful value constellation for users with an ecosystem of services and providers through Official Account and Mini-Programs, WeChat created 22.35m job opportunities in 2018 alone.[101]

WeChat has put the user experience first and in doing so has created an ecosystem with an enormous amount of value for its partner businesses and brands. Rather than just offer advertising, which in fact is minimal on the app relative to other social or e-commerce apps globally, they created a powerful ecosystem where businesses could sell direct to consumers, own and manage their relationship with consumers, creating a frictionless experience for both the businesses and users to access the goods and services they need for their daily lives. Founder Zhang noted in 2019, "WeChat has reached one billion users, but actually we've never thought that the number of users was particularly important... we care more about how to provide our users with more services. This is a more important question."[102]

The value constellation WeChat has created continues to scale and grow, with some eye-popping performance metrics:

- By the end of 2021, there were 450m daily active users of WeChat Mini-Programs, a 15.2% growth from the year prior,[103] which the company believes is a key reason monthly

---

101. Birkinshaw et al., "Innovation and Agility at Tencent's WeChat".
102. Birkinshaw et al., "Innovation and Agility at Tencent's WeChat".
103. Zhenpeng Huang and Sarah Zheng, "WeChat App Keeps Growing Despite Beijing Crackdown", Bloomberg, January 6, 2022. https://www.bloomberg.com/news/articles/2022-01-06/tencent-s-wechat-app-keeps-growing-despite-beijing-crackdown

active users grow as well – as utility increases, so does the user base.

- As of March 2022, the monthly active users of WeChat globally have increased another 30%, reaching 1.3bn.[104]
- The number of Mini-Programs by overseas merchants grew by 268% since 2020, with online commerce transaction volume exploding by 897%.[105]
- Monthly active users of WeChat Search jumped to 700m in 2021, up 40% versus year ago.[106]
- WeChat Pay employees have grown 3x since 2016, reaching 1,200 people, with the service now featuring more than 1,800 bank and financial institution partners.[107]
- Livestreaming e-commerce sales on WeChat grew by 15x in 2021.[108]
- WeChat's WeCom, launched in 2016, the enterprise version of the app intended to support businesses in digital transformation with video streaming, communication and messaging services, reached over 180m active users with more than 10m companies in 2021.[109]

WeChat has effectively become the operating system of daily life in China, used by 80% of the population and occupying 30% of

104. Statista, accessed September 1, 2022. https://www.statista.com/statistics/255778/number-of-active-wechat-messenger-accounts/
105. Huang and Zheng, "WeChat App Keeps Growing".
106. Huang and Zheng, "WeChat App Keeps Growing".
107. Huang and Zheng, "WeChat App Keeps Growing".
108. Huang and Zheng, "WeChat App Keeps Growing".
109. Tencent Press Release, "Tencent's WeCom Sees User Growth Amid Capabilities Integration With Other Tencent Platforms", January 14, 2022. https://www.tencent.com/en-us/articles/2201273.html

the time people spend on their smartphones.[110] WeChat's reach outside of China continues to grow, with users predominantly in Asia. Venture capitalists and investors report that WeChat is a model that innovators in India and Africa are trying to learn from in order to potentially transform their own societies and economies.

Hema and New Retail Create a Powerful New Value Constellation for Grocery

"The era of e-commerce will end soon. In the next decade or so, there will be no such thing as e-commerce, there will only be New Retail," said Jack Ma in 2016 when introducing the Alibaba Group's New Retail strategy.[111]

At a time when businesses were talking about O2O (online to offline) – which was about driving consumers into physical retail from online experiences – Ma described a grander vision. His vision was a fully integrated universe of offline and online retail, enabled by data analytics and artificial intelligence to create a seamless and frictionless world for consumers to access goods and services. This vision represented an entirely new value constellation for consumers and retailers, both of whom would ultimately benefit in the digital retail revolution.

While to some it may sound like a Chinese version of "omnichannel" retailing, the way New Retail sets itself apart is the innovation around customer experience and delivery as well as the scale and speed of service and implementation which leverages new

---

110. Roel Wieringa and Jaap Gordijn, "The Business Models of WeChat", The Value Engineers white paper, March 2021.
111. Wengshou Cui, "Hema: New Retail Comes to Grocery", International Institute for Management Case Study, Lausanne, Switzerland, 2019.

and emerging technologies as enablers to transform the industry. New Retail acknowledges that consumers experience the retail world holistically and that the constructs of offline and online are business and brand constructs rather than helpful frames for consumers. Today consumers interact with brands and experience their products and services across a variety of channels, typically purchasing in the channel that is most convenient for them. Consumers do not mentally delineate the places or occasions of brand interaction or purchase and the expectation is that wherever they seek to experience a product or brand, it is there in a frictionless, seamless fashion for them. Brands that require even a small additional effort to purchase are often forgone for another brand that makes it easier to experience and purchase.

New Retail asserts that traditional retail-reliant brands must integrate online brand experience and purchase, while digital-native verticals should conversely consider physical experiences and purchasing for their customers. To realize the potential and ambition of New Retail means to recognize how consumers today live and that businesses must respond with digitally enabled customer journeys that deliver unique, memorable, and frictionless brand and shopping experiences. Alibaba Group sought to achieve this with their new grocery experience called Hema, which launched in 2016. Hema, known in English as Fresh Hippo, was created as a lab for Alibaba Group to experiment with new approaches and technologies that would ultimately shape and define New Retail.

At the time, grocery seemed an unusual choice for a New Retail experiment. The model was fraught with challenges such as managing cold storage logistics while maintaining profitability – fresh products need different temperatures and many fragile or oddly shaped items are not stackable. Additionally, there was a dilemma in the industry on whether to use physical stores or regional warehouses for distribution and order fulfilment. Using retail stores was expensive as it relied on individuals in local stores to manage the fulfilment process. Further, product availability could not be guaranteed as physical stores sometimes faced stock-outs from foot-traffic shoppers. On the other hand, operating regional warehouses represented an incremental set of cost structures around inventory and logistics – large expenses in an industry where margins are notoriously slim.

Facing these challenges, large overseas players struggled to crack the integration of offline-to-online in grocery. Marks & Spencer in the UK acquired a 50% stake in online grocery retailer Ocado with a view to expanding its online capabilities, while Amazon in the US acquired premium grocery retailer Whole Foods to achieve a physical retail presence.[112] It was precisely for this reason that Alibaba Group sought to explore New Retail in the context of grocery – imagining that if the challenging problem of digitalizing grocery could be cracked, the vision for New Retail could be realized in other contexts.

The China grocery market, though, was quite different from the US or Europe. A whopping 73% of shoppers bought fresh foods like meat, eggs and produce at neighbourhood wet markets, whereas only 22% bought through supermarkets and 3% through e-commerce.[113] Consumers desired the freshest food possible, and it was a habit to purchase daily at the wet market – either early in the morning or on the way home from work – feeling that wet markets provided the freshest foods, because they were restocked daily, straight

---

112. Cui, "Hema: New Retail Comes to Grocery".
113. Cui, "Hema: New Retail Comes to Grocery".

from countryside farms. Supermarkets were viewed by consumers as places to buy packaged foods off the shelf, whereas e-commerce was typically used to buy heavy or bulky products such as laundry detergent, drinks or toilet paper and have these heavy items delivered straight to the door. However, given the rising middle class and increasing disposable income in China, particularly in megacities such as Shanghai, Beijing and Guangzhou, Alibaba Group saw an opportunity to upgrade the consumption and grocery habits of middle-class, urban working consumers who would be open to a more convenience-driven offer.

The first Hema store opened in Shanghai's Pudong district in January 2016 with little fanfare. This first store was seen as a laboratory in which Alibaba Group could quietly experiment with the concept. Six months later, with the model proven, Hema began to roll out more stores across China. The Hema model featured innovative, signature concepts like a live seafood market with an integrated restaurant where the seafood selected by customers could be prepared by chefs, and directly eaten on site. Waiters and sometimes robots delivered these fresh dishes to customers who, impressed with the quality, often then purchased more seafood to take home. This space featured large and exotic seafood such as 5 kg (11 lb) Alaskan king crabs, which attracted many photographs and videos, becoming a viral phenomenon on Chinese social media. As seafood is expensive in China and represents wealth and prestige, the integrated fresh seafood market-cum-restaurant experience became a draw for domestic tourists travelling to Shanghai or Beijing. Independent social media blogs and vlogs even detailed Hema travel and shopping tips for visitors.

Other brightly coloured and lush fresh products were displayed close to the door to attract consumers. All fresh products featured Hema's Full Traceability Program. Consumers could scan a QR code to trace the source of the products and determine, to the exact minute, when they left the farm. Other information available included the temperature of transport, the route, suppliers' official government certifications, and even recipes and customer reviews. Hema launched a private label brand for produce that was colour-coded, featuring a different colour packaging for each day of the week so consumers would know this was today's product, and that yesterday's products had been removed.

Stores themselves had few service staff outside of the restaurant as they were almost completely digitalized, with product information and pricing on barcode shelf tags and a completely cashless checkout process enabled by digital payments. Most staff on the floor were those fulfilling the online orders for which the local store served as a distribution centre.

When ordering online, orders of fresh products were guaranteed to arrive within 30 minutes, with no minimum order – the only restriction was that the order be within a 3km radius of the store. This model not only represented unmatched convenience for the customer, who had only experienced 3–4-hour delivery windows for other fresh good suppliers, but it was also a cost-saver for Hema as it meant that fresh products could be delivered using only insulated boxes and bags, with no need for a cold storage supply chain. Hema even introduced a night service of health and medicine products with the same guaranteed 30-minute delivery in Shanghai and Beijing.

To meet the 30-minute delivery times, orders were prepared in store within 10 minutes. Thanks to the digitalization of inventory, the digital purchasing channel (whether app or web) only presented real-time available products to the shopper, so stock-outs or gaps in fulfilment were deftly avoided. Baskets on an overhead conveyor belt system moved through the store with a computer navigating the basket's quickest route to complete the order. To ensure quick retrieval of goods, order-picking staff were specialized in one area of the store and equipped with a terminal with a digital read-out of the order so that they were ready and waiting when the basket reached the docking station to place the goods inside. Not only was this efficient but it also represented another form of in-store experience and engagement for the shoppers in the physical store as they watched online orders being fulfilled.

With 18 months, 13 stores in three cities were opened that enjoyed 3–5x sales per unit area versus other area supermarkets; Hema reported an unheard-of 35% conversion rate on the app; and 60% of all orders were from the online channels.[114] Customers made 4.5 purchases per month on average, shopping 50 times a year.[115] All interaction with customers was captured in data which enabled Hema's artificial intelligence engine to make product recommendations, advise of relevant promotions and improve delivery service on an individual customer level. Further, internally, data helped ensure that at every store, the products most sought after locally were always fresh and available, and helped the store manage inventory more carefully such that there was minimal spoilage and wastage.

Hema additionally built strong relationships with suppliers, promising no slotting fees, ever.[116] They also formed partnerships

---

114. Glenn Taylor, "Alibaba Supermarkets Blend Offline and Online Via Mobile-First Strategy", *Retail Touchpoints Magazine*, July 26, 2017. https://www.retailtouchpoints.com/topics/omnichannel-alignment/alibaba-supermarkets-blend-online-and-offline-via-mobile-first-strategy
115. Taylor, "Alibaba Supermarkets".
116. Cui, "Hema: New Retail Comes to Grocery".

with provincial government agriculture departments to help them develop methods for higher and more profitable outputs for the farmers, facilitating economic development in rural areas. This behaviour was disruptive in an industry where high slotting fees were the norm and back-door deals were often a necessity for suppliers to secure distribution. These partnerships enabled Hema to build strong private label brands comprising 10% of its sales, a remarkable shift in a market where private label was not popular (as consumers preferred branded products for quality assurance) and in other retailers only comprised 3–5% of sales.[117]

While the planned expansion slowed in 2020 and 2021 due to the pandemic, by 2022, Hema boasted approximately 350 stores in 27 cities across China, targeting dense urban centres with populations of over 1m.[118] Hema's data-driven model, supply chain management and supplier partnerships formed a powerful value constellation which enabled higher margins compared to typical grocery stores. The business operated with higher sales per square meter and less wastage, and delivered better consumer convenience, creating a sticky shopping experience that generated consumer loyalty. As of January 2022, Hema's high-tech grocery model was valued at US$10bn[119] and the business was innovating with a new, smaller format of store, called Hema Neighbourhood.

117. Cui, "Hema: New Retail Comes to Grocery".
118. Jing Zang, "Hema Becomes China's Largest Retailer for Ready-to-Eat Avocados", Product Report, December 22, 2021. https://www.producereport.com/article/hema-becomes-chinas-largest-retailer-ready-eat-avocados
119. Bloomberg News Wire, "Alibaba's Fresh Hippo Said to Mull Funding at $10 Billion Value", Bloomberg.com. https://www.bloomberg.com/news/articles/2022-01-14/alibaba-s-freshippo-said-to-mull-funding-at-10-billion-value#xj4y7vzkg

How to Export This Catalyst

Think of your business as part of a broader ecosystem. By architecting value constellations, you will be able to explode the business's utility and potential reach, because when users' or customers' needs are better met by a solution, product, or service, that business can scale and generate massive social and economic impact.

See the Challenge Through Both Context and Object Lenses

In the West, we tend to follow linear processes and focus on analyzing and categorizing objects using formal logic and rules. China, however, embraces the power of interconnectedness and networks, which enables Chinese businesses to see the broader context and interdependencies that will make a new technology successful. They leverage these network connections to generate value in new ways.

To Chinafy, look through both lenses, the Asian lens of context and the Western lens of object. Zoom into the details via object focus and zoom out for context focus to see the entire picture with a broader perspective. As it is not the natural inclination in the West, pay special attention to the context – interdependencies, contradictions and potential linkages (and even own personal networks) – that could generate value for business by helping to architect a powerful ecosystem that delivers true value to the user.

One you have identified the relationships, networks and connections that have the potential to touch, enhance, or potentially even detract from the user experience, map the ecosystem – identify the relevant players that might have a role to play in how your customer experiences your offer. What barriers or obstacles exist in its usage? How can the experience be enabled or become even more frictionless? What actors or agents might benefit from being part of the offer and therefore represent partnership opportunities?

For example, as we saw in the case of WeChat, Tencent observed that mobile providers opposed WeChat offering free texting, seeing it as a threat to their business – but by helping mobile providers see the bigger picture and opportunity of selling data, they were able to bring the mobile providers on as part of the enabling value constellation to help speed WeChat's adoption. In fact, sometimes bringing the opposition on side and creating a win-win scenario can be the most powerful piece of the value constellation.

When both lenses are applied to map the environment, understanding both the object and the context enables entrepreneurs and managers to become systems builders, assembling meaningful configurations for powerful value constellations that better serve consumers and drive sustainable growth.

Think Grand Design Instead of Technological Superiority

By all reports and analysis, there is no component of WeChat that demonstrates technological superiority. The same is true for Alibaba's Hema. What is unique among both innovations is the assembly of features and functionality based on a vision or a grand design. In both cases, these happened to be based on a founder or creator vision of what the innovation could be that was personally steered every step of the way by that individual and their vision. This is markedly different from the more structured approach to innovation which often prioritizes R&D-led or user insight-led approaches that seek to achieve technological superiority.

An analysis presented in the *Harvard Business Review* found that the grand design approach can be more effective than the standard design thinking approach under certain conditions, particularly when a market is in its early stage of development – and points to other examples of grand design like Apple's iPod and iPhone which were driven by Steve Jobs's vision for a new user experience and in fact did not use any new-to-the-world technologies but rather assembled existing ones in new ways.[120]

Both Hema and WeChat are classic examples of grand design in that strong individual visionaries both directed their development down to the smallest detail. For example, it was Jack Ma's vision for New Retail that drove grocery as the key point of entry as a torture test for the vision – with Hema's tech-enabled grocery retail innovating a totally integrated online and offline experience. On WeChat, founder Zhang insisted that navigation be super simple from the beginning and that "WeChat shall always have a four-icon bar, and never add anything to it".[121] Despite the increasing complexities of features, payments, Mini-Programs and more, the four-icon bar remains unchanged, and the development team was tasked to find other ways to refine user navigation of the super app.

In architecting value constellations, it can be tempting to throw a bit of everything into product features, or cultivate many partners, or even expand into new service or product areas – but innovators must beware diluting the vision of the grand design. Look to ensure what is added is coherently and holistically aligned with the bigger vision of the service, product or offer, and say no to anything that is not. For example, a distinct difference between WeChat and other messaging or social apps is that there is no way for a message sender

---

120. Julian Birkinshaw, Dickie Liang-Hong Ke, Enrique de Diego, "The Kind of Creative Thinking That Fueled WeChat's Success", *Harvard Business Review*, October 29, 2019. https://hbr.org/2019/10/the-kind-of-creative-thinking-that-fueled-wechats-success
121. Julian Birkinshaw et al., "The Kind of Creative Thinking".

to see when or if a message has been read. Zhang felt that "social interaction should have a threshold and when I know if you have received a message, it pressures me to respond".[122] Zhang simply did not see this feature as coherent with the design and operating logic he had in mind.

Use the vision for the grand design as a guide and be selective in assembling the value constellation. Breadth of ecosystem or offer is not a mandate for inclusion. What should be considered most importantly is: what is the value the innovator seeks to create, and is this partner/feature/offer coherent with the vision for that value?

Finally, what both WeChat and Hema illustrate so beautifully is that a vision and grand design can indeed trump technological advancement – as existing technology can be used to innovate, and even disrupt, when clustered in new value constellations to architect meaningful shifts in the economy and society.

Align the Key Performance Indicators (KPIs) Around Value

When looking to architect new value constellations, the initiative and its early success should be measured in terms of creating the best, most useful product for users, not necessarily on more typical business or growth measures of success such as traffic or profitability. This means the KPIs should be different, such that they enable focus on the right system-building activities.

Zhang recalls the early days of WeChat where there were no KPIs at all, explaining, "The typical company goal is to produce traffic and monetize it, so KPIs are designed for this. But when you operate with such a goal, the primary objective is no longer to produce the best product but to try everything to obtain traffic. This is

---

122. Birkinshaw et al., "Innovation and Agility at Tencent's WeChat".

not the principle we advocate for. We want to advocate for the utilization of WeChat to become a good product for our users... to be honest, WeChat never targeted KPIs. Look at Mini-Programs as an example – we didn't know how to establish KPIs for that product."[123] With Mini-Programs being one of the more transformational features of the app and even of the economy in China, one wonders how it might have taken a different shape if the focus were on financial or traffic KPIs.

When thinking about grocery as a point of entry for New Retail, it was an unusual choice to experiment with a retail channel that was already fraught with challenges in its attempt to go digital globally and furthermore suffered from the slimmest margins in the retailing industry. This was clearly not a segment of the industry that would have been chosen based on attractiveness from a profitability point of view. That said, it was an important problem to be solved for consumers and the industry on how to drive convenience, access to high-quality foods, delivered in good and fresh condition, and all at a reasonable and market-competitive price. Therefore, the early KPIs were about delivering value to the consumer – exceeding consumer expectations on delivery speed and convenience combined with a clear assurance on quality based on the freshness and traceability of the food items. Hema did not challenge itself to make a profit in the early days of the business as their focus was on how to architect the value constellations that would meet or exceed consumer needs; once they found this sweet spot, they shifted to managing for operational efficiencies and scaling.

---

123. Birkinshaw et al., "Innovation and Agility at Tencent's WeChat".

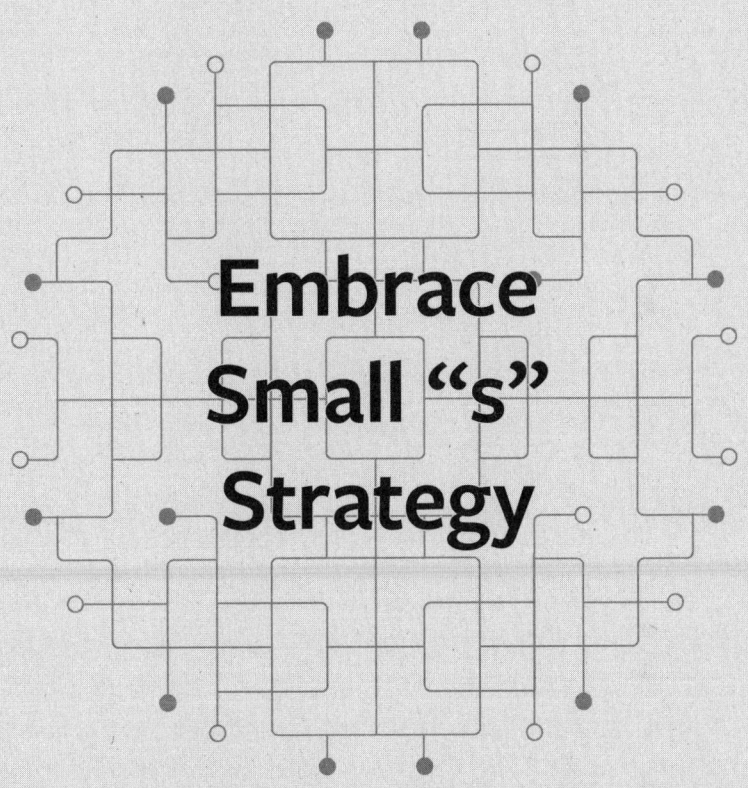

Chapter 7

Embrace Small "s" Strategy

CATALYST 5

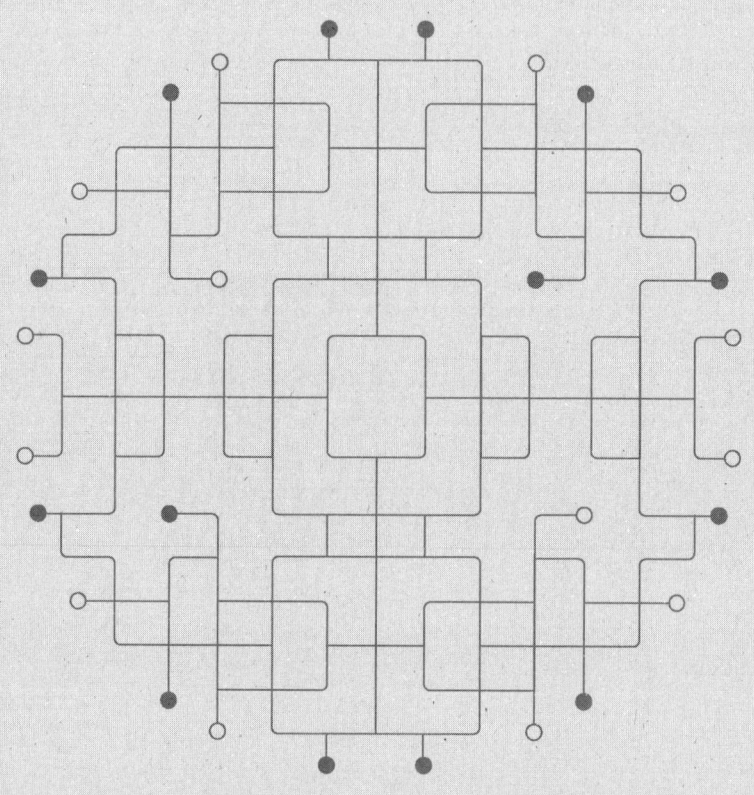

MANY BUSINESS LEADERS spend a great detail of time in the space of deep thinking – exploring how to best capture and articulate the company's purpose, how this manifests in the company culture, and eventually boiling all of this big picture visioning into strategic frameworks for meaty, detailed five-year plans. This is what we would call big "S" strategy. Strategy with a big "S" goes from broad to narrow and can effectively be thought of as strategy from the top-down. In fact, the traditional model for business strategy and planning in the West takes a practicable shape and path:

- Step 1: Craft a purpose and vision for the company.
- Step 2: Develop strategic pillars to support that.
- Step 3: Break the strategies down into discrete tactics to achieve the overall vision.

Chinese businesses, on the other hand, tend to focus on small "s" strategy. Strategy with a small "s" is the field of operational agility, systems support and the everyday routines that translate into how businesses get things done. Small "s" strategy is bottom-up and is often seen as of secondary importance in the Western context. However, most business leaders in China will say that a primary focus on big "S" strategy is self-indulgent unless the small "s" strategy is already in place to make it happen.

Chinese businesses rely less on big "S" strategy as they experience the markets to be emergent and dynamic. China moves fast

– competitors enter, exit and pivot with mind-blowing speed, such that five-year plans rarely have value. What happens in one year in China might easily be a 7–10-year stretch in Europe or the US. Big "S" strategy in China is often not more than a 1–2-year plan, if that. Realistically most businesses and CEOs lead with a vision and generally skip strategic planning as they have found it does not necessarily lead to better outcomes. Instead, they push their organizations to focus on delivery and execution.

With the focus on the front lines of business, everyday routines and behaviours in the business become increasingly more efficient and iteratively improve on business model execution to accelerate growth. This pragmatic focus on small "s" strategy in China makes businesses nimbler and more responsive, able to both answer the larger aims of the business and respond to market or demand changes as well as competitive moves. It is the backbone of innovation, enabling a business to maximize an innovation's commercial potential by getting it to market faster and with wider availability to enable rapid building of scale. Ultimately, in China's ever changing business environment, cultivating small "s" strategy is simply a more critical determinant of success than big "S" strategy. As the rest of the world continues to speed up, business becomes increasingly turbulent, complex and hyper-competitive, small "s" strategy – or the strategy of how things get done – will gradually determine which businesses succeed and which fail. This is why building capabilities and scaling them through small "s" strategy should be at the top of every CEO's priorities.

Creating the World's Largest Appliance Company

Haier is the Chinese appliance company that has been the world's largest "white goods" company since 2011[124], manufacturing and selling washing machines, refrigerators, air-conditioners and much more in over 100 countries. But the business was not always successful. In fact, it was in total disarray until a new management philosophy and focus on small "s" strategy changed its fate.

Haier was established in 1949 as a refrigerator factory in Qingdao, a coastal port city in eastern China more famous for the Tsingtao brand of beer. By the 1980s, this state-owned enterprise, then called Qingdao Refrigerator Co., was mired in debt and teetering on bankruptcy. However, when China opened to the world in 1984, joint ventures were formed between Qingdao Refrigerator Co. and European manufacturers to bring in the latest technologies and thinking. With the infusion of new technology and new leadership under CEO Zhang Ruimin, the company, renamed Qingdao Haier, started to reverse its fortunes.

Nothing in Zhang's past prepared him for this role. Born in the village of Laizhou, Zhang was unable to attend university due to Mao's Cultural Revolution. Instead, he educated himself, reading Shakespeare and the Taoist philosophy of Lao Tzu. In the late 1960s he became an apprentice at a government-owned metal-processing factory and after experiencing some success there, became the manager of a local appliance company. Eventually he was given the failing refrigerator factory of Qingdao Haier to manage. When Zhang

---

124. Paul Leinwand and Cesare Mainardi, "Creating a Strategy That Works", *Strategy + Business*, August 2016. https://www.strategy-business.com/feature/Creating-a-Strategy-That-Works

arrived, he found workers who were not only unmotivated and careless in their work, struggling to make just 80 refrigerators a month, but also undisciplined in habits, often urinating on the factory floor.

Zhang sought to eradicate the complacency of government bureaucracy and rejected the multi-layered corporate hierarchy suggested by Western partners. What he saw was a company with low engagement, low morale, and inferior products which he believed to be linked to a distinct lack of ownership by the employees in what got done and how it got done. Instead, information flowed up to management and the government and directives flowed back down – most people were "just following orders" which were not specific or even helpful operationally as the stakeholders had no real working knowledge of refrigerator manufacturing. He felt that to turn the business around, there needed to be a seismic culture shift – individuals needed to have ownership of outcomes and as a collective they needed to focus on the business of why, what and how things got done, building better processes that would lead to the output of quality products. And most importantly, this all needed to happen in service to the customer or end user.

In 1985, following a customer complaint about a faulty refrigerator, a frustrated Zhang famously ordered employees to destroy over 75 refrigerators deemed to be of unfit quality. Armed with sledgehammers, stunned employees followed the directive, smashing the inferior refrigerators. Grabbing a sledgehammer himself and striking the final blows on the refrigerators as well as the existing company culture, Zhang declared it was time for a change and ushered in a new era of relentless focus on operational excellence and quality.

By 1988, the Chinese government encouraged Zhang to acquire five more failing local appliances businesses, thereby extending Haier into spaces like washing machines and air-conditioners. The company's performance was so impressive that in the 1990s, American conglomerate General Electric (GE) made overtures to acquire Haier. These were rejected by Zhang and instead in 2016, Haier purchased the global GE appliances division for US$5.4bn.[125]

As Zhang developed as a leader, he brought a new approach to Haier, blending traditional Chinese culture with the modern Western business concepts learned from the European partners. This approach evolved into his own unique ideology known as "Rendanheyi". Translated, "ren" means "people" and refers to individual employees, "dan" means "order" and refers to the needs of individual users, and "heyi" means "combination" and refers to the shared connection between individual employees and the needs of individual users. Rendanheyi seeks to simplify hierarchical organizational structures in a belief that layers of hierarchy create distance between the business and the end user, and therefore prevent the business from truly understanding the end user and solving their needs. Instead, Rendanheyi promotes a flat and entrepreneurial organization that encourages decision-making and risk-taking around a common organizational goal: to better solve end user needs.

It is not only a consumer-centric strategy, but also a strong competitive strategy that allows the business to stand apart with differentiated innovations. When successful in identifying a unique set of user needs, Haier also effectively removes itself from competitive comparison as they offer models with features that no other brand does. For example, in 1996 when a farmer complained that

---

125. Press Release, "GE Agrees to Sell Appliances Business to Haier for $5.4B", GE, January 15, 2016. https://www.ge.com/news/press-releases/ge-agrees-sell-appliances-business-haier-54b

his Haier washing machine kept backing up, the repairman sent to check the device realized it was being used to wash potatoes as well as clothing. A new machine model was quickly designed with buffers in the drum to protect vegetables, as well as wider pipes that wouldn't clog. It turned out the market for a washing machine with this functionality was huge, not just in China but in many other countries.

Over time, the Rendanheyi approach eliminated over 10,000 middle management jobs and resulted in the formation of more than 4,000 microbusiness units on an open platform, effectively creating an ecosystem of small businesses and small business "owners" who were incentivized to operate on the level of small "s" strategy – deciding what gets done and how it gets done, all in service of satisfying the end user. Zhang says, "Traditional brands focus on the upgrading of products, but we focus on the iteration or upgrading of user experiences. For example, for the smart home, if users can derive constant value from a set of solutions, they will pay ten times, if not more, than the price of a single home appliance."[126] And for every new solution or product that is imagined, a new set of internal structures, processes, and operations needs to be created and organized. Haier does not operate in the same way as many manufacturers with fixed production lines that can only accommodate incremental product changes.

When asked to reflect on this transition from top-down, big "S" strategy, and hierarchical management structures, Zhang said,

---

126. Zhang Ruimin, "Shattering the Status Quo: An Interview with Haier's Zhang Ruimin", interview by Aaron De Smet, et al. for *McKinsey Quarterly*, July 27, 2021. https://www.mckinsey.com/business-functions/people-and-organizational-performance/our-insights/shattering-the-status-quo-a-conversation-with-haiers-zhang-ruimin

"Several leaders I spoke to, including the CEO of IBM, told me this transformation would be impossible... but we did it. The transformation, and inverting the pyramid, has been achieved, step-by-step, over 12 years. It created a lot of internal conflict because we needed to change our processes from the standard waterfall approach to parallel processing."[127] Today the ecosystem continues to evolve while focusing on the core principles – always promoting collaboration, cross-pollination and connecting all parties to iterate on how to get things done to meet the constantly changing needs of users.

Zhang was the first Chinese business leader to speak at Harvard Business School in 1998, and today, he is a legend in global management circles, known as one of the world's foremost modern leadership strategists and scholars. Haier Smart Home now owns a range of brands including the Whirlpool and Electrolux brands and makes a myriad of smart home appliances in the IoT space and is valued at US$41bn and ranks #405 in the Fortune Global 500.[128]

Cool, Not Cold: Small "s" Strategy in Action

So how does Rendanheyi and small "s" strategy bear out in practice at Haier? Within Haier, the small business units, or ecosystem micro communities (ECMs), are in direct contact with users. The sole purpose of ECMs is to create solutions to satisfy unmet user needs that have been identified. Once they identify a need, these small working teams of 8–10 members are nimble, quickly focusing on what needs to be done and how to get it done. Essentially these teams are

127. Zhang, "Shattering the Status Quo".
128. Fortune Global 500 ranking, 2021. https://fortune.com/company/qingdao-haier/global500/

reconfiguring operations with every project, which would seemingly create chaos in the system, but because the organization operates with what is effectively small "s" strategy, all teams have deep operational expertise and know how to get things done. The benefit, Zhang says, is, "New development cycle times shorten dramatically. What once took half a year can now take a couple of months or less. Collaboration is essential, because if they fail to create value for the users, they don't get paid at all... the only boss in our EMC approach is the user. Everybody keeps an eye on user demands."[129]

The EMCs organize freely around a compelling problem that they all agree needs solving. There's no broader company strategy they are serving, such as "Innovate to grow in the home heating and cooling business unit"; instead EMCs need to find a meaningful problem that can generate strong commercial potential. One such problem was identified by engineer Lei Yongfeng[130] in home air-conditioners. In 2012, Lei discovered a common customer complaint – air-conditioner units blew too cold, which customers thought to be unhealthy and found to be uncomfortable. Lei pulled together a team which was ultimately to produce the Tianzun (meaning "heaven" in Chinese) air-conditioner.

In the traditional structure of innovation in most companies, the product idea may come from marketing-sponsored market research, or it may come from R&D-driven breakthroughs. In either case, in typical innovation projects there is a discovery process that originates in one team and incubates there before it is handed over for the next stage of development. The process is generally

129. Zhang, "Shattering the Status Quo".
130. News Release, "Zhang Ruimin's Haier Power", Haier, April 22, 2014. https://www.haier.com/global/press-events/news/20140426_142723.shtml

sequential and siloed, meaning that the product concept or execution is often fully formed before it moves from ideation to execution. At Haier, products start with identifying a need to be solved and then all members of the team who have various disciplines bring their skills to bear on solving the problem.

In the case of the Tianzun air-conditioner, it all started when Lei got on his laptop and put a simple question out to the social media channels where Haier engages with the 30m[131] Chinese consumers that subscribe. Lei asked, "What do you want in air-conditioning?" The 670,000 responses that followed let Lei know he was on to something – air-conditioning was a space where there were clearly pain points and unmet needs. In China, air-conditioners are used year-round, for heating and for cooling, so nearly every modern home has one. However, Lei discovered that most were only using the heating function; the chief pain point of the cooling function was that most air-conditioners blew too cold. In Chinese culture cold temperatures are considered bad for health. Even cold water is not consumed; it should be room temperature or lukewarm according to Chinese traditional medicine. On top of that complaint there were others, such as units being too noisy and concerns that in pushing around air they were just recirculating environmental dust, which was a key concern in 2012 when pollution was at its peak in China. Also, there were fears that dirt and bacteria could live within the units, making them more likely to spread disease. Finally the free-standing units were large and obtrusive in the home – many the size of a refrigerator – and consumers felt they were unsightly and nearly impossible to conceal.

---

131. Bill Fischer, et al., "The Haier Road to Growth", *Strategy + Business*, April 27, 2016.

The Tianzun air-conditioner set out to solve these pain points. Rather than be constrained by the manufacturing specifications of the air-conditioners that Haier was already making, the EMC set out to build something completely new from the ground up. The team knew if they could demonstrate a use case with a strong business case, they could find a way to get it made and get it to market. The resulting unit was a slim-line column unit with a porthole in the centre – it looked and worked like no other air-conditioner on the market. The porthole served as a wind tunnel, pulling in air from the room and mixing the air from the unit and the room, so the resulting air was less cold. The unit also has air filter functionality measuring the particulate level in the air; this is visible in the porthole, which features lights which glow in different colours depending on the air quality level. As the air is cleaned, the colour changes from red to blue. Finally, the Tianzun linked up to an app which enabled users to start the unit remotely, say before leaving work so that when they arrived home, it would be a comfortable temperature.

What's remarkable about the product, aside from its innovative features, was the focus on cross-functional development and permeability across functional areas. As marketing was thinking about the launch plan and communications, procurement was seeking resources, parts and suppliers for various components, manufacturing was simultaneously working through the production requirements, and finally customer service was also developing their playbook for after-sales service. As these managers worked together in parallel, they also shared across lanes, addressing any disconnects when they arose. This meant the product went to market in half the time as the traditional process where each function would pass its work sequentially to the next function.

Not only that, to ensure no detail was missed along the way, all functions engaged directly with the consumer to check at every step that the product in development would truly close the gap with these unmet needs. All elements yielded a strong feedback loop with unparalleled responsiveness between functions within Haier as well as with the consumer. Eventually the product was launched with the slogan, "Cool, not cold", taking the consumer insight directly into the marketing campaign. The Tianzun set a one-day sales record for air-conditioners in China when it launched in 2013.[132]

Overall, the strong focus on operational excellence and cross-functional permeability means Haier is geared to produce high-quality products at a very low cost through the systems which are continuously improved and constantly evolving, driven by learnings and the internal competition between the EMCs.

How to Export This Catalyst

While big "S" strategy is important in setting the agenda, a strong focus on the small "s" strategy up-levels operational agility, which often results in better products with more commercial impact. Small "s" strategy makes your business more competitive, able to respond to the market with agility and capture opportunity. So how do Chinese companies enable small "s" strategy?

Spark Problem-Solving with Permeable Organizational Structures

Unlike Western companies – which are more traditionally hierarchical, with business units of like products which contain siloed

---

132. News Release, "Zhang Ruimin's Haier Power".

departments of functional expertise – Chinese companies are more transversal, often without separate business units, and relatively flat organizations with regular exchange between levels as well as groups with different functional expertise. In this way, organizations and functions are structured with permeability as a built-in way of working and can transcend the limits of functional boundaries – and building scale rapidly depends on transcending the limits of functional departments.

So rather than typical project management where development moves sequentially with one department handing their completed task to another department to layer their inputs on, the Chinese approach has more interactions at various stages by all departments. These companies know that solutions do not always fall neatly within functional silos and are often generated and sparked through the collective problem-solving that permeable organizational structures facilitate. For example, a typical product development project in a Western company moves through a stage/gate process where R&D completes the product design, then hands it to supply chain for scaled manufacturing, next it goes to marketing to decide the consumer and benefit messaging, and finally on to sales who brings it to the various channels and distributors for sell-in. Each department is effectively siloed and has its own key performance indicators (KPIs) that it is incentivized to achieve. Whereas in China, sales might input at the R&D stage to define the specifications that they think would increase the sell-in potential. Each department has engagement and involvement at each stage which serves to make incremental improvements in the offer that drive operational agility and more often than not, increase commercial potential. And importantly, the KPIs are shared and are generally tied to implementation and sales revenue.

This may mean that in management it is necessary to experiment with different or looser organizational structures or other ways of working that increase the cross-pollination and co-creation potential of the business's functional teams.

Focus on a Few Small "s" Strategies

Operational excellence and capabilities is a wide area, depending on the complexity of your business, probably too wide to do everything at a world-class level. To Chinafy, focus on a few distinctive capabilities that the business will be world-class at. Among the day-to-day business of how and what gets done, identify those areas that will have the most impact on the business and focus on a few select areas.

Distinctive capabilities are not easy to build. It takes time and requires financial commitment and focus. However, with that focus, consistency in these capabilities will be built, and when measured by KPIs every team member will understand what the expectations are and what good looks like. Over time, with consistency, these distinctive capabilities will become competitive advantages.

Encourage a "Try and Do" Mindset and Launch in Beta

Teams that are encouraged to experiment, test hypotheses and structure feedback loops – either with other functions or with consumers – tend to arrive at better outcomes. An effective feedback loop that is common in China is launching in beta. While this is common in the rest of the world in the tech community, it is a concept that has not permeated most other industries. However, in China, brands from soft drinks and footwear to home appliances and electronics embrace launching products on a small scale, for example in e-commerce, pilot trials, test market, or limited editions.

This allows businesses to evaluate the product or offer on a small scale so that teams can learn as they go, continually improving the launch execution and increasing capabilities for the long term, thus providing the necessary insights to scale up for a more impactful launch.

Adjust KPIs to Measure What Drives Small "s" Strategy

Organizations that focus on small "s" strategy can quickly redirect their people and priorities toward value-creating opportunities. It is a common misconception that stability and scale must be sacrificed for operational agility and flexibility.

The traditional measures of success in most companies are growth, profitability, and market share as it relates to the larger organizational goals. While these are no doubt critical measures, they are generally measurements of big "S" strategy. Thus, if businesses want to build a focus on small "s" strategy, then KPIs need to reflect this. This means that processes and time cycles should be measured if responsiveness or speed to market are goals. If quality improvement is a goal, then zero defects could be a KPI.

In general, there are a few best practices to keep in mind. Whatever the KPI, it should be a measurement that becomes part of the daily conversation. It's not just a number but should capture the concept of what the business is trying to facilitate or achieve and should enable conversations about how to accelerate in this dimension or remove obstacles for further improvement. There should be multiple KPIs to avoid the problem of tunnel vision, as relentless focus on a single KPI might drive unwanted behaviour if not balanced with other complementary KPIs. Finally, the KPI should be easy to capture and understand for everyone – that way it truly has the potential to guide and shape the behaviours and actions of the team.

However, organizations should still be mindful of the guiding big "S" strategy and not become let the KPIs become the tail that wags the dog. We see, in the case of Haier, the guiding principle was better serving customer needs, but the business let the working teams define how exactly to do that and set their own KPIs accordingly.

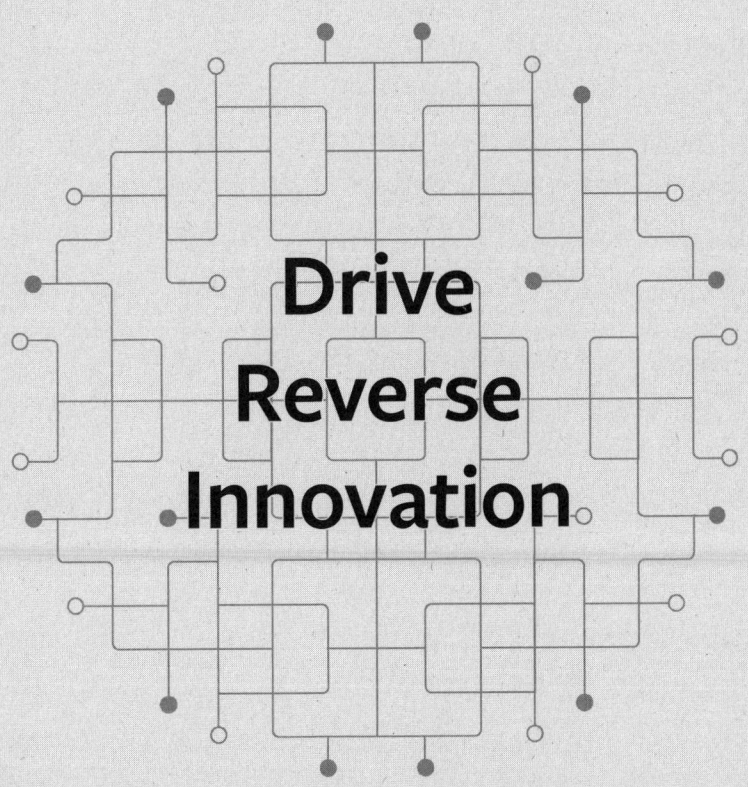

Chapter 8

Drive Reverse Innovation

CATALYST 6

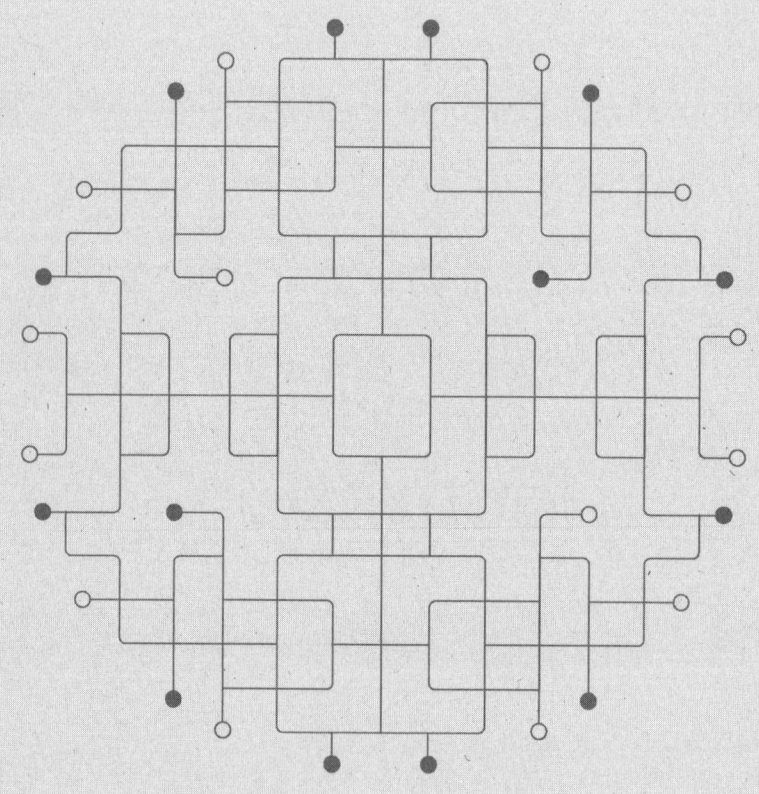

MOST WESTERN COMPANIES innovate to improve upon existing offers and products, effectively funnelling customers into
upgraded offers and higher levels of spending. Amazon Prime
monthly subscriptions and the Nespresso home coffee machine are
some of the more iconic examples of up-trading and premiumization
in recent times. This trend is largely driven by the fact that the average middle-class consumer spend globally for goods and services
has largely been maximized by availability. Thus the pervasive view
is that the simplest and most cost-effective way to grow is to get
existing consumers to spend more on new, premium innovations,
because recruiting new users can be costly and slow to build as it
likely requires different communications and new channels.

It's a model that makes intuitive sense to us, but it fails to take
advantage of the lucrative opportunities that exist at lower levels,
as well as the opportunities to provide services for customers who
desperately need them. Developing countries like China have done
this out of necessity, using a process known as "reverse innovation".
The idea of reverse innovation is to first create and innovate for
the emerging, less-developed economy, often with stripped down
or "good enough" product offerings, thereby mining the gold at the
bottom of the socioeconomic pyramid while also increasing quality
of life for this segment of the population.

"Reverse innovation" is a term coined in 2009 by Vijay Govindarajan, the founding director of the Center for Global Leadership

at Dartmouth's Tuck School of Business in the US.[133] Govindarajan, known as "VG", is widely regarded as a visionary in the field of strategy and innovation. Originally from India and inspired by his own insights of the developing world, he introduced the concept of reverse innovation to General Electric. The core principles are to first create and innovate for the emerging and less-developed economy as a distinct and unique business opportunity, and then secondly to find applications for the cost-reduced alternative in the established and developed economy, unlocking new opportunities with the lower-cost product for new use cases with new user groups. The simplified, lower-cost product thus generates entirely new revenue streams from both types of markets across potentially multiple new user groups. VG describes reverse innovation as "value for many" as opposed to "value for money".[134]

Because reverse innovation focuses on simplified, stripped-down or "good enough" offers, it can deprioritize one of the central tenets of product development – the pursuit of high-value patents and intellectual property. Patents generally require large investments of time and money in research and development but are seen as worthy investments as they often yield strategic competitive postures, high market value, and defendable legal positions that block competitive entry. However, the practical value of any patent is ultimately reflected in market performance and commercial success for the business. The concept of reverse innovation shifts this paradigm, suggesting that defendable patents and new discoveries

---

133. Ariel Tung, "Reverse Innovation to Define a New Phase of Globalization", *China Daily*, August 6, 2012. http://usa.chinadaily.com.cn/epaper/2012-06/08/content_15488024.htm

134. TedX Talks, "Vijay Govindarajan: Reverse Innovation", YouTube, published March 2012, accessed July 2021.

are not the only key to unlock success. Finding a low-tech solution for the masses with a high-value customer proposition can generate even larger market opportunity, opening up new users and new use cases.

This introduces a whole new opportunity to multiple types of business. Businesses that are R&D driven, say medical or biotech industries, could employ two streams of innovation – disruptive and reverse. Whereas businesses that are not heavily invested in discovery and disruption can leverage existing solutions. For these organizations, instead of the pressure to invent and discover, R&D is charged to build upon existing open technologies and solve real customer needs with simpler, more affordable solutions. To paint this is in sharper relief, it is possible that companies with little to no long-range R&D investment could ostensibly be market makers and shapers, transforming entire industries and doing so with potentially outsize profits relative to competitors with sizable, long-term investments in R&D.

Medicine for the Masses

A remarkable example of reverse innovation is GE's Electrocardiogram or ECG machine. The model made and sold in the US was $50,000 for the machine with a custom printer. In 2010, when looking to grow in markets like India and China, GE quickly learned that most hospitals could not afford this equipment. Further, medicine in countries with large low-income populations looks very different. Most of the population live in rural communities with the sophisticated hospitals being in more modern urban areas. The practice of hospitals sending doctors into the villages for visits is becoming more common with a view to increasing access to care. This however comes with additional challenges in that sophisticated diagnostic equipment is not portable, and even if it were, electricity is largely not available in the villages. Thus, diagnostic capabilities outside of the hospital are limited.

GE innovated to solve these challenges by creating a portable, handheld, battery-powered ECG machine for $500 that weighed less than eight ounces and printed on small and widely available calculator roll paper. Easy to operate, with only a green button for on and a red button for off, this simple device transformed the ability to diagnose and treat cardiac conditions in the villages. Today, the portable ECG is sold in 150 countries worldwide and has found a market in developed countries too, largely with emergency responders. In the US, it is now standard equipment in ambulances and firetrucks, resulting in lifesaving diagnostics that enable more precise treatment in the field, which saves lives. Subsequently, GE in China did the same with a portable ultrasound machine, making it fully functional with a laptop unit and reducing the cost from $100,000 to $15,000. This ultrasound machine is now sold in 100 countries, including the US.[135]

Where some companies like GE in the developed world are embracing reverse innovation, most are not. Many multinational businesses, when entering less developed markets, either attempt to adapt or localize their existing global portfolio for emerging markets or aim to trade up consumers to the global product. This continues to limit their potential to succeed or even effectively enter markets with large, low-income populations like China. Consider a product designed for a US consumer with an average income of $66,144 (2021 data), how can it even be profitably adapted for a consumer

---

135. Tung, "Reverse Innovation".

with one-tenth the annual income? In China, where the per capita national income is RMB32,189 or approximately US$4,966 (2020 data),[136] reverse innovation is oxygen for both consumers and the economy.

As Chinese businesses embrace reverse innovation, they can and do travel and decimate brands and products in the West, because who would not choose to buy a quality product that meets their needs at a significantly lower price? Essentially, these businesses create locally, for the domestic market of China, and have demonstrated the potential to win globally.

Smartphones and Smart Living Democratized

Xiaomi is a smartphone and technology company founded in Beijing by serial entrepreneur Lei Jun and six associates in 2010. Lei had previously founded several other technology companies which had proven successful and were later sold to global companies like Amazon. Today, over a decade on, and with Lei still at the helm, Xiaomi is the world's second-largest smartphone maker and a powerhouse player in the Internet of Things (IoT), present in over 100 countries with an annual revenue of $48bn, a market value of $60bn, and over 33,000 employees worldwide. It is the youngest company, in position 338, on the Fortune Global 500 list. For a frame of reference on size, Xiaomi is comparable in market value to any one of the following companies: Uber, General Motors, Colgate-Palmolive, or UBS bank.

---

136. Statistics, People's Republic of China, Household's Income and Per Capita Expenditure in 2020, January 19, 2021. http://www.stats.gov.cn/english/PressRelease/202101/t20210119_1812523.html

Yet when this leader of smartphones and devices entered the market in 2010, it did so with software, offering a free operating system (OS) for Android phones. The OS added more sophisticated functionality in the Android platform, such as a more intuitive interface, cloud backup and storage as well as a better music player. While they did build a loyal following with the OS, Xiaomi realized that they needed their own device to truly demonstrate the potential of the OS. Thus, the first Xiaomi phone was created and within seven years Xiaomi became a global player in smartphones, eclipsing established players like Samsung in sales.

So how did Xiaomi accomplish this in a fiercely competitive market dominated by both local and international players such as Huawei, Lenovo, Apple, and Samsung? Leveraging the concept of reverse innovation, Xiaomi made a more useful product, for more people, at a better price. The Mi One smartphone launched direct to consumers (DTC), stripping out costly distributors and dealers, offering "quality technology at an affordable price".[137] CEO Lei said, "We must curb our tendency to be greedy."[138] Xiaomi embraced razor-thin 5% margins on its smartphones, much less than the industry standard of 20–50%. Yet, the phone was elegant and attractive, bringing some of the design sophistication of Apple to Android users while the functionality of the phone was based on the most used, most-valued features of smartphones such as an intuitive interface, internet browsing and camera functionality.

---

137. Haiyang Yang, et al, "How Xiaomi Became an Internet of Things Power-house", *Harvard Business Review*, April 26, 2021. https://hbr.org/2021/04/how-xiaomi-became-an-internet-of-things-powerhouse
138. Yingzhi Yang, " Xiaomi CEO Lei Jun's Rather Counter-Intuitive Success Formula: Don't be Greedy", *The South China Morning Post*, April 9, 2019. https://www.scmp.com/tech/article/2140644/xiaomi-ceos-rather-counter-intuitive-success-formula-dont-be

Xiaomi immediately grabbed the attention of Chinese consumers with a strong value proposition, and the consumers responded with demand that outstripped supply. This prompted Xiaomi to limit e-commerce sales to one day a week, which in turn generated a media storm which further broadened the brand's reach to new consumers and intensified demand.

But this was not yet getting the Mi One smartphone to the consumer base in China that would ultimately unlock the greatest potential. Following its initial success in e-commerce, Xiaomi sought to expand beyond middle-class, urban consumers. Rural consumers outnumbered urban consumers in China, yet e-commerce was not highly penetrated in rural areas, mainly due to a lack of broadband infrastructure and the inability to afford expensive smartphones to access high-speed data for internet. Thus Xiaomi opened its own neighbourhood brick-and-mortar stores to reach this market and created a system of microloans for purchase, putting smartphones in the hands of rural Chinese consumers. In these lower-tier markets, the price/value proposition was even more compelling, enabling many consumers to purchase their very first smartphone and join the 4G digital and e-commerce revolution that was just starting in China.

The value proposition was also attractive for the consumer smartphone market in India. While the competition looked different, the consumer needs were the same – a low-cost, well-functioning smartphone for the lower-income masses to enable access to mobile internet due to lack of physical infrastructure. When launched in India in 2014, the anticipation for the affordable Mi 3 was feverish and on the day of launch, heavy traffic crashed the FlipKart e-commerce website, India's equivalent of Amazon. Within three years of launch, the Mi brand became the best-selling smartphone brand in India and today enjoys annual sales of over US$9bn.[139]

The Mi 4 is the best-selling smartphone in history, and with a strong position in the smartphone market globally, Xiaomi is seen by many as only a smartphone company. However, Xiaomi saw an opportunity to leverage this winning formula of accessible pricing, most desired features for a "good enough" product, and a sleek minimal design aesthetic across other tech lifestyle product areas. They saw the opportunity for a connected lifestyle ecosystem with a smartphone at the centre as a hub. The breakthrough product was China's first affordable air purifier. Today Xiaomi produces hundreds of IoT products ranging from smart treadmills, electric scooters, drones, TV's, laptops, headphones and speakers to smart watches, water purifiers, kitchen appliances, robotic vacuum cleaners, lighting systems, and beauty and personal care appliances and gadgets. Buying into the ecosystem as a whole has a user benefit in that the Mi phone is an omni remote control for all Mi devices that is more frictionless than other smartphones thanks to the unique Xiaomi Android-adapted OS known as MIUI.

Much like with its smartphones, Xiaomi has introduced this ecosystem of smart products and smart homes to scores of users who would otherwise not be able to afford the more expensive "standard" options in IoT categories. It is no exaggeration that most homes in China have at least one Mi product. That said, Xiaomi as a brand is not perceived as cheap, or for lower-income consumers who cannot afford more expensive brands. It is a highly desirable brand with die-hard fans, one that is known to deliver value for money,

---

139. Counterpoint, India Smart Phone Market Share, February 8, 2022. https://www.counterpointresearch.com/india-smartphone-share/

reliable products and appealing design for users at any income level. Xiaomi further rewards its fans with earlier access to new launches and upgrades, to create further stickiness within their ever-expanding ecosystem.

Xiaomi's cumulative average growth (CAGR) of gross profit over five years is 68.6%. Compare this to Apple's five years' gross profit CAGR of 11.1% and the potential of reverse innovation for economic impact becomes self-evident.

Chinese EV Poised for Global Domination

BYD, or Build Your Dreams, is the Chinese vehicle and transport company many are unlikely to have heard of today but are likely to be driving one of its electric vehicles (EVs) in five years' time. BYD started as a small 20-person outfit, making rechargeable batteries for mobile phones. Within 10 years, it captured half of the world's mobile battery market. Today BYD has more than 22,000 employees, with 30 industrial parks across six continents, making electric buses, monorails, and EVs – all of which are underpinned by their rechargeable battery technology and expertise. Chances are, if you have ever been a passenger on an electric bus anywhere in the world, you were on a BYD, which is the #1 manufacturer in the world and makes one out of five electric buses globally.[140]

BYD already dominates the EV market in China and is poised to dominate globally. BYD entered the automotive industry with its acquisition of Tsinchuan Automobile in 2003. Based in Xi'an,

140. Editorial Staff, "The pandemic doesn't stop the European e-bus market: +22% in 2020", *Sustainable Bus*, February 19, 2021. https://www.sustainable-bus.com/news/europe-electric-bus-market-2020-covid/

Shaanxi province, which is better known as the home of the historic Terracotta Warriors, Tsinchuan was an automotive manufacturer with one key model known as the "Flyer", an economical, compact, five-door hatchback launched in 2001. Rebranded the BYD Flyer 2005, it became the company's first conventional automobile. By 2008, the company had parlayed its rechargeable battery technology into the automotive venture and launched its first EV. The world's first mass-produced, plug-in hybrid car had a longer-lasting battery than other vehicles and was cheaper than anything else being made in the United States or Japan. As the world's first vertically integrated EV manufacturer – making two of the most expensive components of EVs, namely the batteries and specialized transistors – BYD is on a path to realizing its ambition to become the world's leading EV company and penetrate the global market with a more accessible, affordable price point for a high-quality product.

To this end, BYD is investing a great deal in innovation to enable more affordable EVs, and it holds more patents than other Chinese automotive industry leaders – remarkable as a latecomer to the industry. And unlike some reverse innovation cases where technology is well established and thus can be simplified, EV technology and battery technology is emerging. In EVs the battery is everything: it determines the distance the vehicle can travel, the weight and thus the efficiency of the vehicle; battery charging time influences the overall utility of the vehicle; and the ability to change the battery for upgrade determines if the vehicle body can be upcycled when new and better battery technology emerges. These are all the core elements buyers evaluate when purchasing EVs.

Much like Google making the Android OS open source, or Microsoft making the Windows OS open source, open source is a key stepping-stone in a technology platform domination strategy.

Being the driver of a dominant industry platform enables the originator to shape and steer where the technology will go, giving the company an edge in the industry and setting the standard for others to follow. A cornerstone of BYD's global ambition is Fudi. Created in 2020, Fudi gathered five companies to sell batteries and EV components to other manufacturers with a goal to drive an industry standard. In particular, BYD aims to sell its Blade battery technology to other manufacturers which has a 75% price advantage[141] versus the current gold standard lithium-ion batteries.

Reverse innovation comes in more obviously in the automotive side of the equation. From a design, structural, style and comfort point of view, BYD is reverse innovating. They have chosen to seek the savings that fund the battery innovation in being "good enough" as a passenger car, employing industry standard specifications but simplifying and cost-reducing in design, materials, and components. BYD has reverse innovated to develop its own engines and gearboxes, two core technologies in auto manufacture that even the biggest Chinese automotive players often rely on their international partners joint ventures for. So while BYD cars are not as stylish, and may not have as many wow factors like super-large touch-screen gadgetry and high-tech design elements like retractable door handles such as Tesla, they are available at $15,000, delivering outstanding value at one-third of the price of an entry-level Tesla. BYD EVs feature leading battery technology, reasonable functionality, and comfort as well as some surprisingly advanced features. For example, BYD introduced remote control technology three years ahead of Daimler

---

141. Gustavo Henrique Ruffo, "BYD No Longer Hides its Strategy to Rule the World", *Inside EVs*, April 9, 2020. https://insideevs.com/news/408757/ byd-strategy-rule-ev-world/

and BMW globally, which enabled drivers to start and stop the car, drive backwards and forwards or turn left and right with no driver inside – perfect for squeezing into tight parking spaces and enabling more comfortable passenger entry. Heating or air-conditioning could be started remotely for the interior to be preheated or cooled before entry, and air purification systems reducing PM 2.5 were standard. All this for $15,000! This is particularly compelling as EVs have typically been at a price premium to conventional cars, but BYD puts EVs and comparable conventional cars at a similar pricing level, which will have the effect of propelling EV adoption worldwide.

Not only that, BYD is partnering with China's ride-sharing app DiDi to develop a specific and even lower-cost model for ride-sharing. When you visit Shenzhen, where BYD is headquartered, a city of 12.6m (about the same population as Los Angeles and New York combined), all the buses and taxis are BYD. The air is clean, and the city is devoid of typical big-city noise pollution; instead the sound of birds chirping can be easily heard. For BYD, reverse innovation is fuelling both cutting-edge innovation as well as new utility and penetration. This will ultimately step-change China's and the world's journey towards more sustainable human mobility and a better quality of life.

In 2008, when BYD's first EV launched, savvy American investor Warren Buffett's Berkshire Hathaway invested $232m, acquiring a 10% ownership stake.[142] As of January 2022, that investment is now valued at $7.7bn.[143] Also interestingly, it is more than 2x larger

---

142. Rey Mashayekhi, "13 Years After Investing in an Obscure Chinese Automaker, Warren Buffett's BYD Bet is Paying Off Big", *Fortune*, March 2, 2021. https://fortune.com/2021/03/02/warren-buffett-investments-berkshire-hathaway-byd/

143. Russell Flannery, "Sales at Warren Buffet Backed BYD Tripled in December Adding to Big Gains by China Makers", *Forbes*, January 3, 2021. https://www.

than Buffett's stake in US-based General Motors. Globally BYD is currently valued at over $100bn, placing it among the top 150 of the world's most valuable companies. With battery know-how and a recent diversification into solar power, there is speculation if BYD will continue its transformation from battery company to transport company to eventually mobility and energy company.

Agriculture Joins the Digital Revolution

Founded in 2015, Pinduoduo is the e-commerce Goliath that you have likely never heard of. It is an agriculture-focused digital platform and app that connects 16m farmers directly to consumers. It is the fastest-growing e-commerce business in China's history, achieving unicorn status two years after its launch, eclipsing the rise of Alibaba's Taobao, which took five years to achieve the same.

Agriculture, in any economy in the world, has the lowest rate of digitalization – yet the products are fundamental to our daily lives. This innovative platform enabled farmers to participate in the fast-growing digital economy in China, widened their access to consumers and generated both greater sales and profits by going direct to the consumer. Consumers, of which there are 741m[144] monthly active users, get access to more variety and better prices thanks to

---

forbes.com/sites/russellflannery/2022/01/03/ev-sales-at-warren-buffett-backed-byd-tripled-in-december-adding-to-big-gains-by-china-makers/#:~:text=Berkshire%20Hathaway%20holds%20225%20million,the%20Hong%20Kong%20Stock%20Exchange.

144. Palash Ghosh, "Pinduoduo Is Now China's Biggest E-Commerce Platform As Billionaire Chairman Colin Huang Steps Down", *Forbes*, March 17, 2021. https://www.forbes.com/sites/palashghosh/2021/03/17/pinduoduo-is-now-chinas-biggest-e-commerce-platform-as-billionaire-chairman-colin-huang-steps-down/?sh=45f8d6ae62b1

the reduction in complexity of distributors, supply chain and logistics, all of which typically take their cut along the way.

The app has a simple, easy-to-use interface specifically designed for those with limited digital app experience. It works on a combination photo-and-video format where merchants can showcase the farms and the produce – from the story of the farm, the growing philosophy, and growing conditions to incredibly detailed photos and information on the produce itself, like how to use it in cooking or even DIY beauty recipes like avocado facial masks. Consumers can buy household-sized quantities of produce to arrive to their homes, fresh from the farm, in 1–3 days' time. Since the platform launched, it has expanded beyond produce to include other branded daily staple goods as well.

An interesting feature of the platform is that it leverages the power of social by enabling users to "pin" an item to their social media feed, inviting their social connections to join in a group buy with highly advantageous pricing. Prices for group-buying can go down as much as 50–75% off the original price based on volume, with groups as small as three people – a big win for the app's consumers who are more price-conscious than brand-conscious. Consumers have 24 hours to assemble a group purchase, bringing a sense of urgency and gamification to the buying experience. With this group sharing and buying component, Pinduoduo has achieved an unheard-of customer acquisition cost of $2 per customer, compared to $41 for Alibaba's Taobao.[145] Livestreaming sales further enhance the experience for both sellers and users. Finally, buyers

---

145. Elad Natanson, "The Miraculous Rise of Pinduoduo and its Lessons", *Forbes*, December 4, 2019. https://www.forbes.com/sites/eladnatanson/2019/12/04/the-miraculous-rise-of-pinduoduo-and-its-lessons/?sh=fb51a11f1300

are incentivized with rewards toward future purchases to post photo reviews of their purchases on the seller's page, enhancing the credibility of the seller and engagement of the buyer. All this user engagement has led to a seven-day retention rate of 77%, which is the highest of any e-commerce platform in China.[146]

Pinduoduo has also invested in "smart" agriculture, making it attractive for younger generations to enter agriculture as a career, instead of the typical urban migration that China has seen in the last few decades in which young people move to cities in search of jobs and a middle-class lifestyle. Further, for a population whose agriculture requirements are growing exponentially, increasing agricultural production is a fundamental national and societal need. To encourage young farmers, Pinduoduo staged a competition in 2020 in collaboration with two national universities and the UN Food and Agriculture Organization for the development of cost-effective technologies suitable for small farm-holders. The technology developed is now in use in tomato and strawberry farming and has enabled small farmers to more than double their management capacity.[147]

To reverse innovate, Pinduoduo assembled existing social, e-commerce and group-buying practices in a simplified and easy-to-use format that enabled a population of farmers and rural consumers, often without internet and relying only on cellular data services, to join the digital revolution. Unlike other e-commerce in China, Pinduoduo taps into an underserved group. Pinduoduo users tend to be in lower-tier cities or in rural communities and skew older,

146. Natanson, "The Miraculous Rise of Pinduoduo and its Lessons".
147. Global Newswire, "Pinduoduo Deepens Agricultural Digital Inclusion Efforts", *Yahoo Finance*, March 21, 2022. https://finance.yahoo.com/news/pinduoduo-deepens-agricultural-digital-inclusion-111200689.html

lower-income, lower-education, and female[148] – in these homes, females are typically in charge of managing the household purchasing. In mining the gold at the bottom of the socioeconomic pyramid, Pinduoduo has helped improve the lives of these communities by providing access to better prices and fresher products and has been lucrative for both farmers selling on the app and the platform itself. In 2018, Pinduoduo listed on NASDAQ as PDD at a valuation of $20–24bn. In 2022, Pinduoduo's market capitalization is nearly $60bn, making it the 280th most valuable company in the world.[149]

How to Export This Catalyst

What principles can be exported from China, based on the success stories of GE, BYD, Xiaomi, Pinduoduo and others, to capture the opportunity that lies in reverse innovation?

Look for Opportunity Among Underserved Populations

In China we see that reverse innovation enjoys outsize commercial success with populations that are underserved. This is contrary to the prevailing business paradigm that suggests the largest commercial opportunity lies in groups of people with higher income and socioeconomic standing. Populations with low disposable incomes or living in poverty are largely ignored by businesses as they are not seen to be commercially viable or ripe markets for innovation. Yet

---

148. Kirk Enbysk, "How Pinduoduo Became the #2 eCommerce Marketplace in China", *ApplicoInc*, 2018. https://www.applicoinc.com/blog/how-pinduoduo-became-the-2-ecommerce-marketplace-in-china/#:~:text=Pinduoduo%20is%20the%20fastest%2Dgrowing,years%2C%20respectively%2C%20to%20accomplish.

149. Companies Market Cap, Pinduoduo, April 2022. https://companiesmarketcap.com/pinduoduo/marketcap/

reverse innovation demonstrates the opposite – this population has a great many unmet needs and is generally more sizable in developing markets. If the needs of these large, underserved populations are meaningfully addressed, with innovations that solve real problems and needs, there is indeed gold that can be mined at the bottom of the socioeconomic pyramid.

While often the needs of this population are thought of as more foundational needs – access to health care, clean water, good nutrition – this does not mean that business cannot play a role in solving these needs, or that foundational needs are the only problems that demand solving. In the case of GE, increasing access to diagnostics does lead to better health care, which is a foundational need and is where reverse innovation has significant impact. But in the case of Xiaomi, smartphone technology is potentially even more transformative in revolutionizing the quality of life for this underserved population by providing them access to information as well as goods and services that would otherwise likely take decades for this population to have proximity or access to.

Embrace Lower Margin Plays

Reverse innovation by definition is a lower-priced, simplified offer that enables penetration and proliferation. Remember Professor VG – this is value for many as opposed to value for money. If a business has an expectation for industry standard margins, they will either be disappointed or fail to reach the launch phase. This does not mean the commercial opportunity is not attractive, but it does mean the name of the game is high volume of sales at lower margins. The aim is to get the product into as many hands as possible for as many different uses and applications as possible. As a result, the margins and resulting profits will look different, and are unlikely to meet other industry standard benchmarks.

Further, to achieve the price point that will enable a reverse innovation to fly, there might be a need to streamline not only the product but also the value chain to realize savings. For example, in the Xiaomi case, the brand went direct to the consumer and did not deal with distributors or sales agents, which was commonplace in the industry. This reduction in value chain complexity led to fewer parties taking a cut of sales, meaning another layer of savings could be achieved and passed on to the buyer in the form of lower prices.

The risk of operating on razor-thin margins is that if any of the components of your product or any elements of your supply chain dramatically increase in price, there is not much of a cushion to absorb this volatility. Take the Xiaomi case, for instance, where the smartphone business was operating on 5% profit margins versus the industry standard of 20–50%. If a significant element in the value chain skyrocketed in price, it would likely strip away profits. Therefore these companies often vertically integrate to have greater control over the critical inputs along the value chain of the product.

Focus on High-Value Utility, Not Just Being Cheap(er)

In China we see that reverse innovation that enjoys disproportionate commercial success is about businesses that focus on delivering the most desired, most utilized features in products, stripping them down and streamlining to essential functions that create the most utility for the user. Cost reduction is an outcome of reduced functionality, and these savings are passed on to the user.

Yet, this is not about cheaper products only, but rather the value equation delivered in spades with utility and desirability. This means that first you need to understand the user and be deeply acquainted with the factors and features that drive utility. For example, in the

Xiaomi smartphone product, most Xiaomi customers were new to smartphones, so the big win was the easy-to-use interface that diminished the new user learning curve. In the case of BYD, it is about innovating to combine better technology with cost-reduced comfort to arrive at a more useful product, thanks to a longer-lasting battery, at an entry-level price point in EVs. Further, as electric cars are not only better for the environment, they are also generally cheaper to own and maintain in the long run as they have fewer parts. Thus, BYD EVs not only convert existing and potential drivers to a new platform but also transform the economy of taxi transport and ride-sharing with low-cost EVs.

Realize the Bi-directional Potential of Reverse Innovation

Going one step further, when businesses reverse innovate, they can often realize two opportunities: the opportunity to mine the gold at the bottom of the socioeconomic pyramid by addressing the needs of an underserved market, and the opportunity to leverage the new offer to capture new users and new usage in either more affluent consumer groups or in more developed and established markets.

Remember GE and the portable ECG device developed for rural communities in emerging markets? This reverse innovation was also transformative for health care in the home market of the US as a portable diagnostic device for emergency responders in the field. Or consider Pinduoduo, which is digitalizing agriculture with a social, gamified e-commerce app that creates a direct-to-consumer channel for farmers. While Pinduoduo initially set out to target more rural users, it is increasingly gaining traction with middle-class urban consumers thanks to its strong value proposition. Further, imagine if this innovation were leveraged in any country in Europe or the US, enabling consumers access to a different kind of produce or foodstuff from what they can get in the typical supermarket, e.g., an app for fresh-from-the-farm dairy or other regional, artisanal food products. The Xiaomi smartphone and IoT case in China demonstrates that lower-cost products can in fact open opportunities for both higher and lower-income consumers within the same market as well as abroad, e.g., in India.

Reverse innovations are able to explode business potential outside of the initial use case. This is why it can and should be exploited bidirectionally; while typically developed for emerging economies, they can subsequently be leveraged to disrupt across multiple user groups and use cases in other types of economies and markets.

Combine Innovation and Reverse Innovation

When disruptive innovation or technological step changes in innovation are combined with reverse innovation, more compelling offers can emerge. Take, for example, the BYD case. There is no doubt BYD is leading an ambitious performance-driven battery innovation programme. This battery innovation seeks to deliver step change functionality to consumers in the form of increased driving time and decreased charging time. But to realize its ambition of becoming the global leader in EVs, the car must be affordable. To make the price accessible, BYD finds opportunities to arrive at a reasonable set of features and comfort that meet consumer expectations. And further, to lead and shape the industry, they make some key battery technology open source to advance the industry itself.

Xiaomi smartphones innovate on the OS to make the Android interface even simpler to use, but then streamline the features offered to provide only the most utilized functionality. This combination of true innovation and reverse innovation generates a winning fusion of desirability and utility at a hard-to-ignore price point.

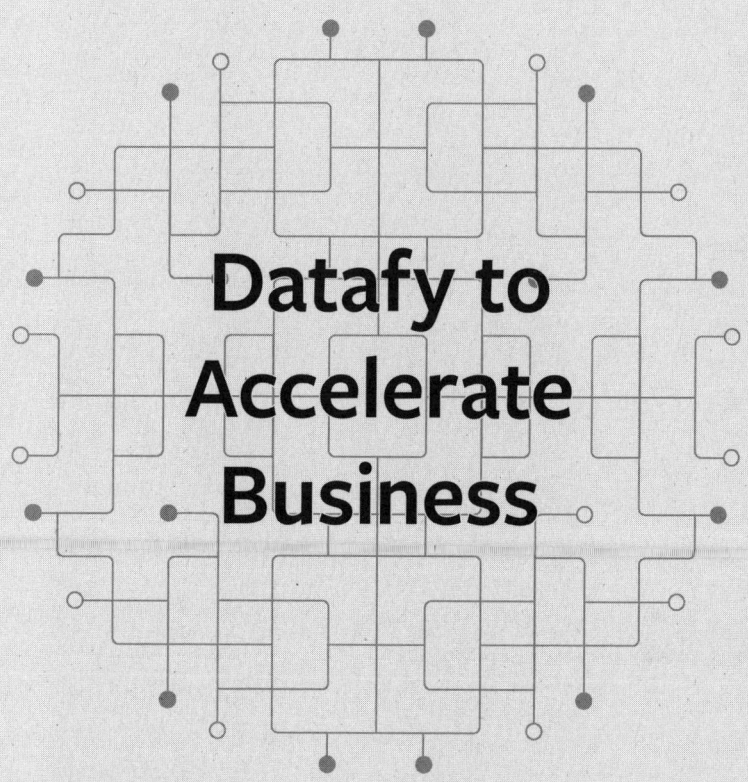

Chapter 9

Datafy to Accelerate Business

CATALYST 7

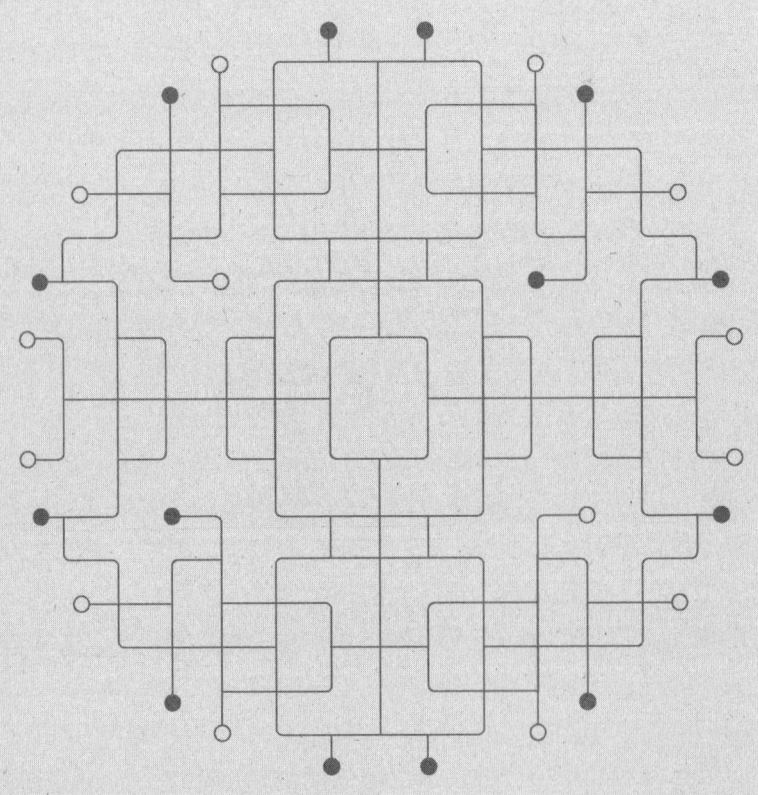

IN CHINA, data has been so thoroughly integrated with every aspect of business that it doesn't require a separate strategy. Data *is* the strategy. This is wholly different from most businesses in the rest of the world for whom data collection and analysis is an arm of the business but is unlikely to be at the centre of the organization.

To better understand the difference between strategy for data versus data as strategy, consider sports.[150] If business were a basketball game, many companies in the United States and Europe play a competitive strategy that is defensive when it comes to data. They use data to analyze the play of the game and movement, and to respond defensively. In this case, the ball is data and your business is reacting and responding to your opponent's moves with the ball on the court.

In business, unlike in basketball, there is a delay in data. For most companies, data comes in weekly or monthly reports. These reports identify and analyze trends, and predict future movements or forecasts based on these trends. When data strategy is defensive, data is a limited historical account of market, competitor, and customer information. A historical perspective is valuable, to a degree. History often repeats itself, patterns emerge, and this information enables businesses to predict the future behaviour of, and defend

---

150. Leandro DalleMule, Thomas H. Davenport, "What's Your Data Strategy?" *Harvard Business Review*, May-June 2017.

against, competitors. But when it is the only approach to data – and for many companies this is the case – it keeps businesses one step behind, consistently in reactive mode. It is difficult for any team or business to get ahead when the game is played this way – and as is the case in most sports, the best defence is a strong offence.

An offensive approach with data is also a strategy for winning, as discovered by many Chinese businesses. Not only winning, but also leaving your competitors so far behind that there is no real potential to catch up. This is because when data is the strategy to win, businesses become omniscient and hyper-responsive to the ever-changing market and consumer needs. Data effectively becomes the engine of business to deliver game-changing performance and achieve sustained competitive advantage.

And this is not just the stuff of tech companies. In fact, data-as-strategy is transforming many non-tech industries in China. Data-as-strategy is most impactfully deployed in areas of business where there is high potential for competitive differentiation – in consumer and customer insight, sales and marketing, and operational efficiency. When used this way, data is less about evaluating outcomes (data as defensive and historical) and more about deciding what can or should be done (data as offensive and real-time). This is data that is used to metaphorically build the car as the CEO is driving it. For example, this is the defining feature of what Alibaba's Jack Ma calls New Retail – and it is the framework of data analytics that all successful businesses will need to be built on to be competitive in the future. In new retail, businesses use CRM, real-time data, and AI to continuously learn about their customers and operations, becoming virtually omniscient about the key dynamics driving growth and profitability.

Tech Startup or Beverage Company?

One such CEO is Tang Binsen, founder of Genki Forest Food Technology Company. Formerly a programmer and gaming executive, Tang saw the opportunity for tech and data to shake up the consumer world after selling his first startup in mobile gaming for US$400m in 2014. He noted that China already had enough strong players in e-commerce, gaming and social, but despite this level of development in digital platforms, there were still many lifestyle gaps in China versus a country like the United States. His feeling was that this was not attributable to a lack of technology, where in some cases China was ahead of the US, but rather to a lack of high-quality local brands. "China doesn't need any more good platforms," Tang wrote in an internal email in 2015, ostensibly referencing the mega-platforms of Baidu, Tencent and Alibaba. "But it does need good products."[151]

In turning his eye to brands and consumer products, Tang observed that of all the large and growing industries, fast-moving consumer goods (FMCG), particularly in food and beverage, were operating on a conventional model where tech and data had yet to be fully leveraged. Tang had no experience with FMCG or F&B, but this is very often the case with Chinese entrepreneurs. What he saw was an opportunity to disrupt consumer products with tech and data know-how. Tang set his sights on beverages with an aim to unseat global behemoths and local market leaders Coca Cola and PepsiCo in China.

---

151. A.J. Cortese, "Beverage Unicorn Genki Forest Wants to be Treated Like a Tech Startup, but Does the Label Stick?" kr-asia.com, April 15, 2021. https://kr-asia.com/beverage-unicorn-genki-forest-wants-to-be-treated-like-a-tech-startup-but-does-the-label-stick .

To do so, Tang employed a data-driven strategy. In fact, Genki Forest's operating model has more in common with a tech startup than with an FMCG company. Genki Forest started by populating an innovation product pipeline, defined by fringe trends starting to emerge on social media. This pipeline of products is teed up and ready to go with beverages slated to be launched in quick succession, a pace typically only employed in the tech world. Release of new products is informed by continuous data mining of sales and trends, which enables new products to be brought to the market at precisely the right moment that a trend is building and can be fully exploited. Factories are leased to ensure flexibility in manufacturing. And not surprisingly, Genki Forest has streamlined the route to market by going direct-to-consumer (DTC), with e-commerce as the dominant channel of sales, skipping the distributor network and typical supermarket and convenience store retail channels. Social media and social commerce are both key marketing and selling channels to build the brand and drive consumer demand. A focus on heavily hyped online shopping festivals and high-profile digital influencers has helped make Genki Forest the best-selling beverage brand in key selling periods, which has further boosted the profile and momentum of its now trend-setting beverages.

In five years, Genki Forest has rapidly scaled, selling its sugar-free soda, milk teas, and energy drinks in China and 40 other countries. Sales reached US$1.2bn in 2020 and the company valuation is US$6bn,[152] based on the highly valued potential of its unique

152. Rui Ma, "Data Driven Iteration Helped China's Genki Forest Become a $6B Beverage Giant in 5 Years", TechCrunch, July 26, 2021. https://techcrunch.com/2021/07/25/data-driven-iteration-helped-chinas-genki-forest-become-a-6b-beverage-giant-in-5-years/#:~:text=The%20bottled%20beverage%20industry%20wasn,outfit%20known%20as%20ELEX%20Technology.

data-driven business model. For comparison, Coca Cola's total revenue across all brands was US$37.5bn in 2020, which gave it a commanding 48% global market share. Genki Forest's valuation is the same size as the global annual sales of Coca Cola Company's Sprite brand, one of the top ten soft drinks in the world by sales, sold in more than 190 countries.

Data-Hungry "New Retail" Makes Fast Food Smart

The proliferation of data means that rather than being product-centric, businesses and brands are able to be increasingly consumer-centric, which has given rise to a unique consumer experience in China. Dubbed New Retail by Alibaba founder Jack Ma, it opens a window into the future for other markets of a truly seamless and frictionless browsing and buying environment that is fully flexible, adaptable, and customizable by the consumer. In fact, the ultimate purpose of new retail is personalization – buy it, have it any way that you want it – which may not involve a traditional retail outlet at all. New retail is data-hungry, and with AI now being layered on top, data for new retail becomes smart, self-learning, and always improving. It is said that if new retail keeps progressing on its current growth trajectory, e-commerce will soon be reduced to a traditional business as new retail replaces it and becomes the dominant consumer experience.

Observe new retail in the unlikely transformation of fast-food or quick service restaurants (QSR) in China. Again, QSR is not a typically tech-heavy sector globally as the traditional business model is reliant on convenient locations, food quality, and consistently high levels of cut-through advertising as key levers of the business. However, in China, data-as-strategy is fundamentally changing the way the game is played, and one company is leading the way.

China's biggest fast-food operation today is Yum China, operators of the Taco Bell, KFC, and Pizza Hut franchises. Yum Brands is American-originated, but in 2016, Yum China spun off and became locally owned. Since this time, Yum China has invested in building a digital ecosystem and harvesting data-as-strategy to emerge as an innovative leader in new retail and data-driven business in China.

The engine of the business is its digital ecosystem of the KFC and Pizza Hut super apps and the 240m Chinese consumers who use them (as of end 2019). The apps provide an immersive experience that makes them sticky and allow the brands to engage with consumers wherever they are on a broad range of topics – not only food but also music, sports, gaming, and entertainment. Within each app are personalized digital features such as coupons and vouchers, privilege memberships, e-commerce, payment options, and corporate social responsibility activities. The data enables a wealth of insights at customer, city, and store level, which helps to drive highly differentiated and more effective store formats, locations and menu items. As digital marketing accounts for 60% of Yum's marketing spend, real-time data powers a flexible yet targeted approach based on consumer preferences. Yum can effectively nudge and guide marketing programmes in real time to build awareness and loyalty faster than ever before. With data-as-strategy, Yum is able to more effectively manoeuvre the key levers in the fast-food business model.

In 2019, Yum went one step further on its innovation-with-data journey in the form of AI-enabled menus and recommendations for each diner, with personalized customer interaction and trade-up opportunities based on local tastes. The AI-powered menu has already boosted average per-order spending by 1% – the equivalent of about US$840m worth of fried chicken and pan pizzas each year.[153]

But data and AI are not just about marketing and upselling. They help Yum China forecast demand, cut food waste, deliver menu innovation, optimize supply chain management, and create delivery and in-store operational efficiencies. For delivery, AI schedules the cooking and preparation time of orders that include both food and beverages, so that the food arrives warm and the beverages cold. An AI-driven dispatching system and logistics overflow support makes the relationship between customers, riders, and stores more frictionless.

Back-of-house operations use AI-based technology to improve sales forecasting, which leads to better inventory management and store labour scheduling. Tailor-made algorithms identify changing data patterns at the store level, such as location, sales performance, weather, promotions, and holidays to enable the quick reallocation of resources to new roles and growth areas. The company is also rolling out smart watches that enable managers to closely monitor the ordering and serving status of restaurants to quickly identify and rectify any issues before they become service bottlenecks.

In store, technology disrupts and makes for an immersive customer experience. Ice-cream is served by robotic arms. Customers can control the background music through their mobile phones.[154] Many stores have no cashiers to take orders or process payment – in fact, you would be hard-pressed to find human beings other

153. Bloomberg News Wire, "Yum China's Bet on AI and Robot Servers is Beginning to Pay Off", March 5, 2019. https://www.bloomberg.com/news/articles/2019-03-05/ kfc-owner-defies-china-slowdown-with-a-i-menus-and-robot-servers
154. Bloomberg News Wire, "Yum China's Bet on AI and Robot Servers".

than customers in the front of the restaurants. Orders are placed on an interactive screen with a chatbot and are completely cashless, taking only digital payment made by AI-powered facial recognition software. Today, between delivery and in-store, more than 60% of orders are made digitally.[155]

Ultimately for Yum China, technology and AI bring precision and personalization to every interaction with the KFC and Pizza Hut brands. Based on its innovative tech-powered approach to transforming food and food service, in 2020, Yum China was named to *Fast Company* magazine's annual list of the World's Most Innovative Companies and was named one of China's 10 most innovative companies. Not many restaurants end up on either list, which is typically dominated by the usual suspects of technology, pharmaceuticals, and startup disruptors.

Since its spin-off from its American parent company in 2016, Yum China has experienced significant growth – in the year-ending March 31, 2021, net income increased by more than 72% over the previous year.[156] Yum China's stock price on the NYSE, ticker YUMC, rose from $28.14 in November 2016 to $61.44 in August 2021.[157]

155. Press Release, "Yum China Named to Fast Company's Annual List of the World's Most Innovative Companies for 2020", Yum China, March 11, 2020. https://ir.yumchina.com/news-releases/news-release-details/yum-china-named-fast-companys-annual-list-worlds-most-innovative

156. Yum China Net Income 2015-2021, *MacroTrends*, accessed April 2022. https://www.macrotrends.net/stocks/charts/YUMC/yum-china-holdings/net-income

157. Yum China Net Income 2015–2021.

Data-Driven Technology Enables
Delivery in Minutes

In the United States and some of Europe, with an annual membership fee of US$119 (as of August 2021), Amazon Prime members can receive delivery of eligible goods overnight. When Prime launched in 2014, this was a massive leap forward in challenging conventional retail that accelerated the fundamental shift to online in consumer buying habits in the United States and Europe. Seven years on from launch, the delivery window for some goods has even shortened to hours with the offer of same-day delivery.

Compare this to China, where delivery is measured in minutes, not hours. In China, it is possible to order from e-commerce or a food-delivery site or app and enjoy a wide variety of goods delivered, on average, within 30 minutes. This could be anything from a basket of groceries to a flat-panel television to a pair of sneakers – even a single cup of coffee can be delivered. No order is too small in monetary value or too large in physical size for instant delivery. Thus, it is not surprising that in the increasingly frictionless shopping universe of Chinese consumers, delivery time has become an important variable in consumer choice. Between multiple apps and order possibilities, the fastest delivery wins the purchase.

This consumer expectation, along with industry promises, has had the unintended effect of creating driver safety issues. As companies attempt to minimize delivery times with timing algorithms and incentive schemes for drivers, drivers sometimes put themselves in harm's way, risking injury and even death. With both public and government pressure to reform delivery practices, alongside customer pressure to shorten delivery times, companies moved to pilot autonomous vehicle delivery in 2016 in a race to shorten the standard delivery time for goods, and to do so safely.

Cut to 2020, where in a pandemic, autonomous delivery proved to be an ideal solution. The pandemic accelerated the autonomous rollout given the need for contactless delivery. The autonomous service, comprising a fleet of self-driving vehicles, was deployed more widely, particularly in Wuhan for contactless delivery of medical supplies to Wuhan Ninth Hospital, Covid-19 ground zero in China. Autonomous delivery by self-driving vehicles was scaled further by e-commerce company JD.com in 2021 to 200 cities with a delivery-in-minutes service. In China's popular 618 shopping festival the same year, JD.com recorded delivering a skin care set by autonomous delivery[158] to a consumer just four minutes after the customer paid the remaining balance of her pre-sale order.

Alibaba's Chief Technology Officer Cheng Li says, "Autonomous driving technology is becoming a core technology in the digital era."[159] Autonomous delivery, which still looks like the stuff of science fiction in most other countries, is now table stakes in the e-commerce game in China. And while the autonomous vehicle delivery innovation is remarkable in and of itself, what makes this technology more than a novelty, and fuels it as a highly commercial application, is data. While autonomous vehicles do deliver more

---

158. Mark Tanner, "Online Delivery in China is Nothing Short of Gobsmacking", *China Skinny*, June 9, 2021. https://www.chinaskinny.com/blog/online-delivery-china?utm_source=news_chinaskinny_com&utm_medium=email&utm_content=The+Weekly+China+Skinny&utm_campaign=20210608_m163525755_20210609+-+3&utm_term=View+on+the+web

159. Monica Suk, "Alibaba Deploys 1,000 Delivery Robots As E-Commerce Booms in China; Accelerates Digitization of Hainan", Alizilla (Alibaba Press Release), June 11, 2021. https://www.alizila.com/alibaba-deploys-1000-delivery-robots-as-e-commerce-booms-in-china-accelerates-digitization-of-hainan/

safely without the need for human operators, effectively address-ing the delivery driver safety concerns, they are not the only key to unlocking shorter delivery times. They do not drive faster, nor are they immune to traffic. Faster delivery times are powered by data-driven systems of smart distribution hubs with hyper-local ori-entation, with goods pre-stocked in anticipation of future orders. Real-time data continuously updates to ensure local distribution hubs have the right type and amount of stock based on time-of-day shopping patterns, neighbourhood demographics, and types of goods commonly needed. This looks a lot different from one neigh-bourhood to the next. Imagine being a family in the suburbs being able to get diapers delivered in mere minutes versus a young urban-ite wanting a trending cosmetic product to change up their look for a night out. Inventory is calibrated with real-time data multiple times a day, resulting in an entirely next-level realization of "just in time" inventory management that enables agility in order fulfilment.

So while driver safety and the pandemic's contactless delivery needs no doubt propelled autonomous delivery to scale, data was the key that unlocked the commercial impact of this innovation in creating tangible value through increasingly frictionless shopping in the form of shorter delivery times.

With Data as Strategy, Fast Fashion Becomes Real-Time Retailing

Unless you are a fashion-forward Gen Z female, you might not have heard of SHEIN (pronounced she-in), the fast fashion online-only company that has eclipsed the ubiquitous Zara and H&M brands. SHEIN is a business developed in China, but it is not intended for the China market. With shipping to 220 countries, SHEIN has its biggest market in the USA, with other strong markets being the EU, Russia, and the Middle East.

In 2021, SHEIN's mobile app exceeded 7m active users a month in the US alone.[160] Google statistics show that users search for it three times more than Western brands like Zara. On TikTok, the hashtag #shein has captured over 6.2bn views. The momentum of this business is staggering – SHEIN has doubled its sales every year for eight years running. So why is SHEIN growing so fast and what makes them different from other fast fashion brands – aside from their laser-focused Gen Z target and online-only model? Three key success factors of SHEIN are changing the game of fast fashion: speed, price, and gamification.

The first factor of SHEIN's success is hyper-speed to market. Speed is, not surprisingly, a central tenet of fast fashion, and SHEIN is operating at a speed unmatched by any other player. For comparison, Zara pioneered fast fashion with inspired-by-the-runway looks in store within two to three weeks. Since the 1990s, this timing has been the gold standard in fast fashion and was groundbreaking at a time when most brands and department stores released new collections seasonally, two to three times a year. The core enabler of the Zara model is their uniquely flexible supply chain based on just-in-time manufacturing principles – a practice borrowed from Japanese automotive manufacturing and applied to textiles and clothing. For fast fashion newcomer SHEIN, while speed is most certainly facilitated through their agile Chinese supply chain (which also relies on just-in-time manufacturing), supply chain is not the

---

160. Daiane Chen, "SHEIN Market Strategy: How the Chinese Fashion Brand is Conquering the West", Daxue Consulting, February 16, 2022. https://daxue-consulting.com/shein-market-strategy/

main lever of speed; data is. Where SHEIN shines is in data-driven customer insights that enable the business to identify and react to trends more quickly and release of-the-moment styles within seven days of trending social media posts. That means if a Gen Z influencer sports a look on TikTok that starts trending, SHEIN has the look up for sale online within the week. With data-driven insights, SHEIN releases 2,000 SKUs a day, compared to Zara which releases 1,000 new SKUs per month.[161]

These data-driven insights are in fact the real engine of the business and are a masterful combined effort of mining trending fashion and style posts on social media as well as their own social marketing activities to generate real-time data on their target audience and product portfolio. SHEIN uses a unique affiliate programme where up-and-coming influencers receive commission for promoting the brand with posts of their outfits. Likes, shares, and comments yield real-time insights. SHEIN partners with celebrity A-listers such as Katy Perry, Hailey Bieber, Lil Nas X, and Yara Shahidi, which yields further insights on various segments and profiles within their customer base. SHEIN also hosts live shows once a week on Instagram, and rather than having a single global Instagram or TikTok account, SHEIN maintains individual accounts by country to understand each market and customer more discretely. All this data becomes actionable insights for spotting trending fashions and styling in the market organically, rather than the fast-follower approach other fast fashion brands employ which relies on inspired-by-runway looks.

Another key lever in the fast fashion industry, and for SHEIN,

---

161. Greg Petro, "The Future of Fashion Retailing: The Zara Approach (Part 2 of 3)", *Forbes*, October 25, 2012. https://www.forbes.com/sites/greg-petro/2012/10/25/the-future-of-fashion-retailing-the-zara-approach-part-2-of-3/?sh=f2c67e67aa4b

is price. Price has always been a fundamental promise of fast fash-ion – the runway look for less. For Gen Z in particular, price is a highly sensitive factor with tipping point potential as the fashion-able Gen Z'er faces the dilemma of having a relatively low dispos-able income but a high desire to have a fresh, of-the-moment look. SHEIN delivers in spades for this consumer: where a summer dress at Zara or H&M averages around US$30, SHEIN delivers a simi-lar dress for half that. In fact, given that the business is born in China, it might be surprising that SHEIN chooses not to compete in its home market. But a US$15 summer dress is not a competitive price in China, which is why SHEIN seeks to dominate the overseas fast-fashion world where it can deliver a price advantage.

Much of the price advantage can be attributed to SHEIN's native understanding of manufacturing in China, which gives them a proximity-based advantage over other global fast-fashion brands also with production in China. Being on the ground, they have developed a unique manufacturing strategy by targeting underper-forming, under-capacity factories with out-of-date inventory man-agement systems and replacing these with the SHEIN data-driven systems in exchange for guaranteed demand. It's a win for both par-ties. SHEIN does not need to own the factories as assets but effec-tively controls them, guaranteeing their supply chain. The factory owners have fully utilized assets and learn how to manage a data-driven business based on real-time consumer preferences, thereby upskilling their operations.

Finally, using learnings from gaming and e-commerce, SHEIN also gamifies the shopping experience, making it extremely sticky and yet another source of data for insight and action. SHEIN's points-based rewards system gives users points for activity and affil-iate marketing. To gain points, users must check in daily or make product reviews, which demands daily active use. Points are also awarded for small tasks like email verification and for bigger tasks like engaging in special challenges, like posting videos of "SHEIN hauls", videos where users purchase many items of clothing and combine them into outfits. Points have monetary value, with 100 points equalling $1 that can be spent on SHEIN. Gamification drives engagement on the platform, which generates data, which generates even more customer and product insights. It is a virtuous cycle of increasing engagement and brand omniscience.

With a data-as-strategy approach applied across all levers of fast fashion, SHEIN has transformed fast-fashion into real-time retail. Today SHEIN is valued at an eye-watering US$15bn, having eclipsed Zara in 2020.

How to Export This Catalyst

In the cases of Genki Forest, Yum China, autonomous delivery in e-commerce, and SHEIN real-time retail, we see that next-level performance for any industry starts with data. When companies use data as offence, they generate more value to consumers and shareholders as they outpace competitors and differentiate their offer, enjoying sustained competitive advantage. So, what guidance can be given for how to export this Chinafy insight and deploy data offensively as strategy?

Get Data Early

In China, it is common to launch offers in beta, which means to bring an unfinished product or offer to market. Launching in beta was not invented in China; it originated in the United States in the software world and was adopted by Silicon Valley startups. However,

China does this routinely and not just in the startup universe. It is the practice of large and small companies, established industries and new ventures. This is because Chinese businesses know that in launching early, the real value is not in capturing early adopter sales or first-to-market position, but in the data. This is as true for beverages and beauty products as it is for fin-tech and apps. Capture data early and iterate your way to perfection, with user insight that likely none of your competitors have. Even if all the kinks are not ironed out, launching in beta helps you assess if you are actually solving the consumer need or problem you set out to solve, thus helping to craft the offer to be more consumer-centric and enabling this optimized offer to scale, typically creating a competitive advantage that leads to larger commercial impact.

For existing businesses or brands, it is also common in China to pre-launch new or updated offers in beta with a small, select group of superfans or influencers. China's ride-hailing app DiDi, which is more than three times larger than its global competitor Uber, routinely launches new features to VIP customers, heavy users of the service. This is not positioned as being a beta tester, but as an offer of exclusivity and hand-selection. In this way, they make customers feel valued and influential while also getting data to improve the offer before scaling to a potentially less forgiving and wider user base for whom a bad experience might lead to brand switching.

While there are most certainly risks to launching in beta, the benefits of early data capture outweigh the potential downsides. But don't misinterpret this to mean that it is acceptable to launch a substandard offer, which is often assumed about China. It is about capturing the data to make the offer even more compelling to consumers. Thus, to Chinafy, bring your offer to market sooner, with a view to iterate and optimize the path to success.

Use Real-Time Data to Drive Real-Time Responsiveness

If you are already in the market, or are going to market, set the business up to capture data in real time. No matter how simple or complex your business, whether you are a major multinational or a local business, seek to capture data with as little reporting lag time as possible so that data can be utilized and acted upon with urgency to drive better outcomes for the business.

This may be in the form of multiple, integrated data systems in the business or a high level of consumer engagement on relevant social platforms. It could even be social listening, following trending topics and hashtags. Whatever it is, be consumer-obsessed.

When businesses have real-time insights, they can unlock a new level of sensitivity to consumers and deliver real-time responsiveness, effectively anticipating consumer needs at every step. And when a business moves from answering consumer needs to anticipating them, it undoubtedly soars past the competition or potentially even creates a new standard in the industry, as we see in cases like SHEIN.

Beware of Becoming Data-Rich and Information-Poor

To Chinafy, drive from data to insights. Failure to do so renders your business data-rich and information-poor. When data is strategy, data must progress from capture to the formulation of insights or information that is actionable for the business. This is when data becomes strategic, accelerating the business and empowering the people guiding the business from insight and information to execution.

This often requires connectivity across platforms and systems to connect the dots to transform data into insights and information. Thus, leaders must consider the overall network of data – what is being collected, by which function of the business, and how the disparate systems and pieces of data can come together to illuminate or amplify one another, resulting in a clear story for the business.

Use Data as Disruptor

The Genki Forest example shows how data can disrupt industries and unseat incumbents. What is most interesting about this disruption is that FMCG world is rife with data – data in the form of monthly sales reports at the SKU and store level, pricing and promotion data, followers and engagement on social media, advertising performance data, eye-tracking data for retail shopping, brand affinity and equity data, product performance data, in-use product experience data... the list goes on and on. The challenge is that much of the data in the FMCG world is backward-looking and is used to inform competitive strategies that are effectively defensive in reaction to what is already happening in the market. While trend reports exist, they are quarterly at best and annually at worst, so it is often not possible to act on them with any sort of timeliness. In effect, whether most FMCGs realize it or not, this approach to business and consumer insights puts their business at a disadvantage. To be on the front foot and use data as a disruptor, this backward-looking data, while still necessarily valuable, needs to be met with an equal if not greater emphasis on forward-looking data. A pronounced emphasis on where consumers are headed is needed.

Anyone with of-the-moment, data-driven insights – even if outside the industry with no experience – can enter and disrupt. Imagine the possibilities if you both know the industry well and could increase your organization's ability to obtain real-time insights. The potential is enormous.

A common counterargument to disrupting your own business

model is cannibalization of the current base business. If the opportunity for disruption exists and you don't take it, someone else will. Better to disrupt than be disrupted. In China, this is where one can observe a pronounced difference in philosophy: there are no immutable truths or concrete legacies. There is a distinct willingness to disrupt and disrupt one's own business if the opportunity exists to do so.

Chinafy with the New Retail Model

Armed with China-style consumer-centricity, real-time data, real-time responsiveness, and a willingness to disrupt, you can Chinafy the customer journey with the New Retail approach. Do not think of your business as offline versus online; embrace the concept of New Retail to imagine what a seamless, frictionless, and personalized customer journey would look like.

It all starts with the concept of convergence of digital and retail, which is of course enabled by data, and is much wider and deeper than the concept of omnichannel in play in the US and Europe. As in the Yum China example, new retail brings together physical, digital, data and technology to make business smart and self-learning, which drives a virtuous cycle of continuous improvement.

In fact, in China, many Western brands are already effectively delivering the new retail experience. Brands from Nike to Louis Vuitton are delivering game-changing new retail experiences, driving brand preference with consumers. What is yet unrealized is the potential to take these China learnings back to their home markets to change the game at home. That said, IKEA recently launched the store of the future in Shanghai (August 2021) as a pilot programme to explore a new retail configuration for the business that could be exported if proven in China.

Democratize Data

Successfully deploying a data-as-strategy approach requires ensuring that the principles permeate the entire organization. It is only when data is democratized that it becomes a key enabler of growth. This means that data should not only be concentrated in the hands of a Chief Technology Officer or Chief Information Officer and their departments. Nor should it be siloed in functions such as Consumer Insight as a capability in the hands of a few. Data helps all parts of a business iterate and improve in real time to better serve consumers and streamline operations to become more efficient, less wasteful, and more responsive. Every element of a business, from marketing to supply chain, can use data to enhance performance. This also empowers managers to nudge the business toward incremental gains that add up to fundamental shifts in performance. Further, beyond departmental silos, business should also consider data concentration and accessibility across levels in the organization. Data should not be limited to those at senior levels, or conversely relegated as an analytical task to juniors who run reports. Data familiarity should permeate the entire organization at every level.

Do Not Lose the Human Touch

Data is information and can help us understand people better, but it should not replace the human factor totally, especially in high-touch, high-value customer service and interactions. For example, in luxury categories, personal service is a fundamental expectation of the buying experience. Unlike the Yum China example, a luxury business cannot rely as heavily on technology and AI to deliver the experience that closes the sale. While this does not mean that data cannot be used to inform the experience and continuously optimize it, data-driven systems are not a replacement for the intimacy of one-to-one selling. In some businesses, human touch can be the ulti-mate personalization of experience, driving not only the current sale but long-term brand affinity and loyalty.

Data is the key to unlocking seemingly unlimited potential in business. With data-as-strategy, businesses can know their users better than the users know themselves! Consumer-stated prefer-ences and behaviour intentions are often contradicted in eventual actions, and actions speak louder than words. As demonstrated in this chapter, data-as-strategy also unlocks operational insights and opportunities that transform efficiency and reduce waste – better for business and better for the world. When brands and businesses Chinafy with a data-as-strategy approach, they become hyper-res-ponsive disruptors poised to transform industries, categories and experiences.

Chapter 10

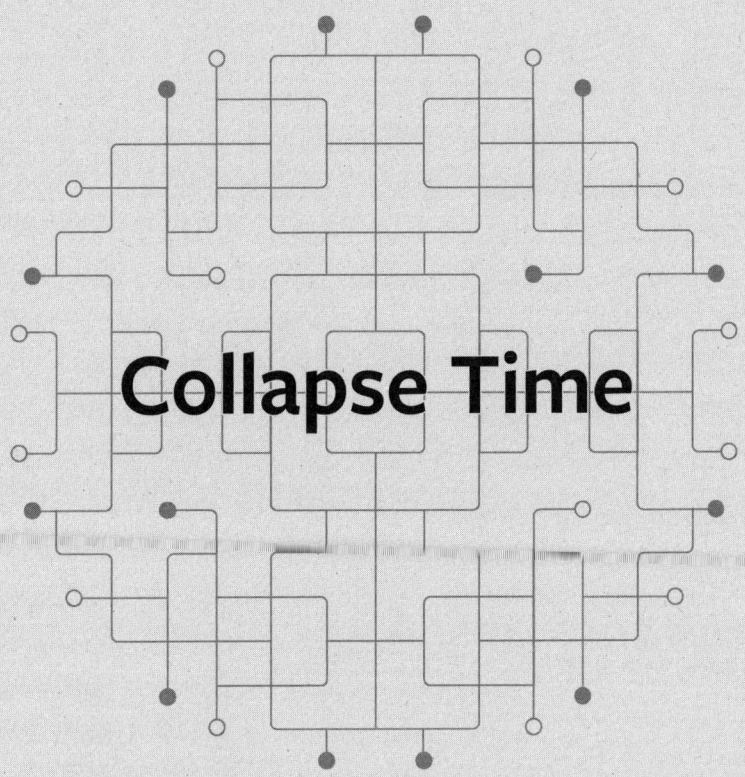

Collapse Time

CATALYST 8

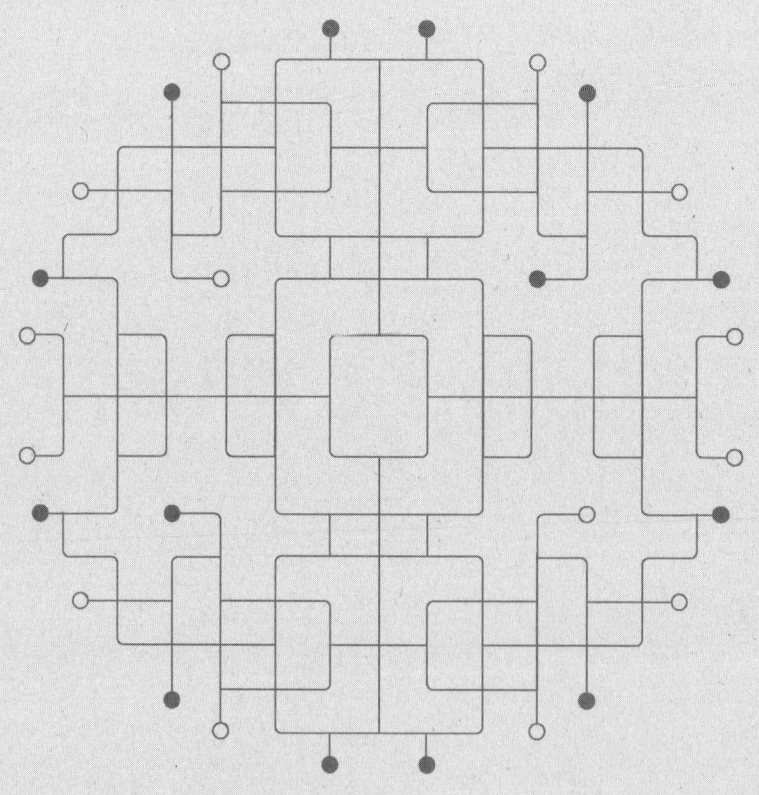

WHY HAS CHINA been able to innovate and grow at the speed it has? An American trend researcher, Zak Dychtwald, founder of the advisory firm Young China Group, set out to answer this question. Considering China's reputation for imitation and a lack of visibility of high-profile, daring entrepreneurs compared to countries like the US, Dychtwald sought to understand what other levers may be facilitating this growth – and he happened upon an unexpected conclusion. It was the hyper-adaptability of the consumer population who lived through unprecedented amounts of change that were driving the speed and scale of innovation. Dychtwald then created the Lived Change Index (LCI) as a measure of this phenomenon. LCI takes available per capita GDP information and compares it to understand the rate of change in a society and how lives may have changed. Take for example, someone born in 1990 in the US versus China. In the US the GDP per capita has increased 2.7x since this person was born. In China, a person born at the same time has witnessed 32 times per capita GDP growth in the same period![162]

There are many factors to GDP growth. Obviously, the starting point of the economy is relevant here – the US was already much better off in 1990 than China. Yet, for reference, other rapidly developing nations like India and Indonesia hover around 5–6 times per capita GDP growth. So at 32 times per capita GDP growth in China,

162. Zak Dychtwald, "China's New Innovation Advantage", *Harvard Business Review*, May-June 2021 Magazine Issue.

imagine the change society has experienced in this time, and not only that, imagine the speed at which it has happened and the adaptability that it has required of society.

Many discount this growth and when discussing the speed of China's growth, there is the common refrain that many hands make light work, and that China's growth can be attributed to a huge population of cheap labour working 24/7 due to lack of labour laws and protections. There is also a common perception that "China speed" is the result of cutting corners and low quality standards. These are not inaccurate, but they are misleading. While these points may have had shades of truth 40 years ago, for the last 20 years these views are outdated and simply incorrect. China's speed and agility is real, quality at pace has been realized, and this can be attributed to the hyper-adaptability of the culture and workforce. Decisions that would take US or European companies weeks or even months can and do turn into action and product prototypes within days in China.

Also, the product development timeline is an area where China has been truly innovative. The typical Western product development process, in consumer goods for example, can take anywhere from 12 to 24 months and involves multiple steps of research and development, product testing, clinical trials, etc. Chinese companies compress this timeline into mere months or even days, putting out hundreds more products than most Western companies. The downside to this strategy is that you may have a high churn of products that don't sell well – so it may appear that time, energy, and investment have been wasted on those products that do not pan out. However, what Chinese companies have found is that you also have a higher number of products that *do* sell well, and you benefit from learning what doesn't work, piloting various strategies in the digital ecosystem and driving continuous user and consumer engagement.

Across many industries, China speed is evident as China blows away standard timelines to get better products to market faster, thereby maximizing commercial impact in any industry in which they play.

Leaving Competitors in the Dust

In mobile phones, Huawei created a processing chip for its innovation Mate 9 mobile phone in just eight months – one-third less time than the global industry standard of 12 months.[163] In fact, the global mobile industry was stymied as to how this was accomplished, considering Huawei was starting from scratch and the phone delivered breakthrough technology at the time.

The Huawei Mate 9 was a feature-packed model at an attractive price and, at the time, the flagship model for the brand. The phone handset was Porsche-designed and featured cutting-edge technology including a machine learning-powered system which monitored how the phone was used and changed the allocation of processing power accordingly. This meant that the Mate 9 actually got faster the more it was used – the opposite of what happens with most Android phones. Its 5.9-inch screen allowed the phone to be used as a mini tablet, providing dual functionality in usage as a "phablet". The device also featured a faster-charging battery that would provide a day's worth of usage with only a 30-minute charge. The Leica camera lens led to higher picture quality than previous phones. Huawei sold 5m units of the Mate 9 phablet in the first four months

---

163. Savov, V., "ARM's idea of 'China speed' helps explain why it's so hard to compete with Chinese phone makers", theverge.com, May 30, 2017.

of sale, 36% more when compared to the sales of its predecessor, the Mate 8.[164]

Huawei's method for designing and engineering the Mate 9 was fundamentally different from the typical approach for development that was widely employed in the industry at the time. No steps were skipped, and Huawei employed the same amount of testing and due diligence. But what they did differently was prioritize both speed *and* quality, which drove development differently and led to different types of problem-solving as well as taking on new risks.

For the Mate 9, the engineers reimagined the steps of the typical project development timeline. Specifically, they started on the phone design before the chip was finished. By taking some educated guesses and expecting certain chip thermal and power requirements, when the chip arrived, the engineers were already well ahead in designing the phone. By parallel-pathing activities, rather than staging them sequentially, the team shortened the timeline by months, leaving any potential competitors in the dust.

The risk of parallel-pathing is that if the engineers miscalculate, the two streams of work may not dovetail seamlessly, and they may have to start over when the chip arrives. In this case, the product would be out in the typical 12-month timeframe and the only loss would be the sunk cost of the parallel-pathing of incremental resources. However, if the two streams did dovetail successfully, the new chip would be first to market globally. Huawei succeeded, and the commercial gain far outweighed the potential risk and expense of the additional resources. Not only that, Huawei reported that they learned a great deal about parallel-pathing and how to further

164. Mitja Rutnik, "Huawei Mate 9 sales reach 5 million in first four months", Android Authority, April 13, 2017.

streamline and de-risk this approach in the future. Effectively, Huawei built a new organizational capability that enables them to achieve even greater competitive advantage.

Sprinting to Success

Foreign companies operating in China have taken notice of "China speed" and are responding with accelerated processes to drive efficiencies of their own to remain competitive.

Nestlé in China is one such example. An innovation sprint process has collapsed the typical innovation timeline from 18–24 months to six months. With this sprint approach, Nestlé is able to be responsive in a fast-moving market where foods and flavours are trend-based and consumers are constantly seeking out, and highly responsive to, innovation. Within a year of implementing this new process, Nestlé introduced 170 new food and beverage products in China, versus 34 the previous year[165], including completely new categories in which Nestlé has not historically been present, for example, Muscle Hunt high-protein water launched in 2019.

The sprint process identifies and prototypes new ideas in just four days with an internal, cross-functional team including colleagues from R&D, Marketing, Sales and Supply Chain, and is broken down as follows:

- Day 1: The team mines consumer information – from existing market research to sales data to trend inputs from social

---

165. Tingmen Koe, "New Product Priorities: Nestlé unveils plan to launch 170 products to market this year", Food & Beverage Innovation Forum, Food Navigator Asia. April 29, 2019.

media and industry reports. Key opportunity areas are identified for exploration and development.

- Day 2: Concepts are co-created by the cross-functional team,
building from the opportunity areas, and moving into product
descriptions, features and benefits. More than 100 product
concepts are usually iterated with copywriting and rough visu-
alization so that the product idea starts to come to life.
- Day 3: The R&D team works to create rapid prototypes for
each of the concepts. Often this involves a prototypical formulation as well as packaging with a view to bring to life the
promise from the product concept.
- Day 4: The concepts and prototypes are exposed to consumers for feedback and learning. The top-rated concepts move
forward for further development and launch.

When products are ready to launch, the aim is to get them to
market as soon as possible. Often this means e-commerce, which is
the fastest route to market versus the typical 1–2-month process of
shipping products to retailers or distributors and having them flow
through to the retail shelf. Early signs of success show Nestlé which
products are worth leaning into with stronger marketing and distribution support. It's entirely possible that some products experience
limited success and never go through to retail. That said, there is as
much learning from what fails as there is from what is successful.
And this knowledge can flow into the next four-day sprint to inform
a more appealing product proposition.

Therefore, the sprints not only enable speedier launches of
incremental innovations but also give Nestlé valuable learning
and skills from doing so, for example upskilling the team on agile
working and co-creation, e-commerce selling and data mining,

understanding consumers and preferences more deeply, refining product expression and presentation for impact – and doing it all at pace. These learnings will enable larger and more disruptive innovations to be landed more effectively in the future – ultimately up-levelling their internal route-to-market capabilities. Following the innovation sprint initiative, in 2020 Nestlé China achieved its highest growth in five years.[166]

Nio Challenges the Automotive Industry

Serial entrepreneur William Li, often dubbed the Elon Musk of China, is the founder and CEO of Nio electric vehicles. Nio – whose name in Chinese, Weilai, means "blue sky coming" – is also often called the Tesla of China. Unlike BYD, another homegrown EV company which produces affordable electric vehicles, Nio plays at the premium end of the market, offering a vehicle that is more lifestyle purchase than functional transport from point A to point B. Drawing from Li's experience as an internet entrepreneur, Nio seeks to build a unique and sticky user experience for drivers of their vehicles, building superfans and aggregating them into a community of users. This is an EV company that also has its own digital currency, a branded line of clothing, multiple clubhouses and showrooms throughout China, and an app that is the hub of the brand. Nio is also the first Chinese car maker to go public on the NYSE, in 2018.

Founded in 2014, Nio has risen quickly to become one of the top players in the EV market in China and is expanding globally.

---

166. Health Products Association Report, "Nestlé's China Revenue Cruises Well Into the Billions", March 1, 2021. https://uschinahpa.org/2021/03/nestle-chinas-revenue-cruises-well-into-the-billions/

With investors including prominent Chinese tech founders such as Richard Liu of JD.com and Tencent, Nio brings cutting-edge mobile internet applications and EVs together to deliver a vehicle to market which is differentiated from Tesla, who is their closest competitor in the premium EV segment. The software, or the mobile internet lifestyle user experience, is just as important as the hardware, the car itself and the battery life which enables longer driving times in EVs. Nio is also differentiated from Tesla and all other EV and conventional carmakers in another way – its speed to market. Nio managed to do something unheard of in the automotive industry, bringing three vehicles to market in three years' time.

On average, from design to manufacture, the development cycle for cars – known as "programme time" – is 48 months, or four years. Programme time is split into three phases. The first phase of programme time is 24–36 months. This is the most intensive phase and consists of designing the vehicle and engineering the various components from chassis to engine to body, as well as rigorous safety and crash testing. The next phase moves the process into manufacturing, where automakers work through how to produce the vehicle at scale, creating or adapting the tooling and machinery to produce the vehicle and identifying the processes to get vehicles off the assembly line with a consistently high standard of quality and low defect rate. The final phase is about building scale in manufacturing while also selling the vehicle into distributors and dealers, preparing the logistics for delivery and shipping as well as creating the marketing plans and campaigns for the launch.

Some companies, like Tesla, have been able to shorten the time frame to 3–3.5 years through a variety of approaches like parallel-pathing or keeping the same underbody of the car (where most of the technology lives) and just changing the upper body from a styling point of view. But vehicle manufacturers, overall, have yet to crack programme times that are substantially shorter. So how did Nio, a new car manufacturer founded by an internet entrepreneur, with no previous engineering specifications to draw from, launch three models of cars in three years?

So first let's talk about why it would be important for a new automotive brand to have a range of vehicles, and quickly. When it comes to car brands, the industry and consumers generally view new brands and their first models with, at worst, skepticism, and at best, a "wait and see" attitude. Concerned about reliability, durability and safety, many buyers prefer to wait until a new car brand is established and proven. Being established means having multiple models on the market with a track record. Thus for any new car brand, the faster a range of models can get to market, the better any individual model's sales are and brand sales overall. Therefore, time is quite literally money in this industry. It is estimated that a four-month delay on any given model can cost a business up to US$2bn in lost revenue opportunity.[167]

As a latecomer to the EV industry, Nio faced several challenges. It had no existing factories or infrastructure for production and no bench strength in design or engineering. It was also one of many Chinese companies – several of them being other automakers with deep pockets and resources – who were racing to capture the market. Nio made three critical decisions which enabled it to start quickly off the blocks and emerge as a leading player in EVs.

First, in terms of investment, it chose to invest in technology development as opposed to building a manufacturing footprint at

---

167. Nico Berhausen, Nick Hannon, "Managing Change and Release" *McKinsey & Company*, March 20, 2018.

the outset. With a founder whose career was shaped in the technology industry, a decision was taken that for a smart EV, the emphasis needed to be on the user experience technology to set the vehicle apart. Nio chose to outsource the manufacture of the vehicle to a local OEM, JAC Motors, thereby avoiding the initial time and costly resources needed to build manufacturing capability. Nio also formed a partnership with Indian car maker Tata, who had expertise with lightweight aluminium bodies – weight being a critical factor in the battery life of EVs. Nio decided to lean into what they felt they knew best, and source best practice from partners.

Secondly, Nio hired and assembled a global team of world-class project managers and engineers with deep automotive experience, relying on their knowledge to navigate the complexities of bringing the software and hardware together in a functional vehicle. By having senior talent in-house, Nio was able to deftly navigate all the workstreams individually as well as bring them together with the speed that comes from a team of experts.

Thirdly, Nio chose to sell directly to consumers, cutting out further lead times of selling in the models to dealers, and reducing the costs to the business. Instead, it sought to develop a curated brand experience that would build superfans at every step of the customer journey from purchase to after-sales engagement and service. Another important part of the customer experience of EVs is battery service and swapping, so Nio focused a significant amount of its resources towards building an infrastructure of more than 300 battery-swap stations all over China. The battery-swap stations were the first of their kind, covering thousands of miles of road in China, and enabled drivers to drive into the station and have the battery swapped in three minutes, less than the amount of time needed to fill a conventional car with gasoline. These key brand and business enablers were built simultaneously while the cars were being designed and manufactured.

Between selecting outside partners with deep functional expertise, investing in the necessary internal expertise for project management and development, and cutting out one part of the process – the dealer sell-in – Nio was able to conquer the previously unconquered limit of the 3–4-year programme time, getting three models to market in three years. They have since launched in the UK and Norway and plan further Western European expansion. As of April 2022, Nio's market value is US$27.5bn,[168] similar in value to the 1931-founded, German Porsche automotive company.

How to Export This Catalyst

What principles can be gleaned from these and other success stories to move at pace and capture maximum commercial potential anywhere in the world?

No Sacred Cows

"Sacred cows" is a colloquial term used to describe ideas or customs held, often unreasonably, to be above criticism. What might a sacred cow be in business? Well, in the case of Nio, it might be that a car brand needs to manufacture all of its own vehicles. In the case of Huawei, it might be that in mobile phones a handset is designed only after the chip specifications are well in hand. A sacred cow in consumer products might be that months of consumer insight work leading up to identifying an innovation, as well as rigorous

---

168. Companies Market Cap, April 22, 2022. https://companiesmarketcap.com/nio/marketcap/

consumer validation in the form of qualitative and quantitative testing, are needed to adequately assess a new product idea for launch. Are you starting to get the picture?

What notions do you hold sacred in your industry that a disruptor might come in and challenge? Unless it is in the space of regulatory or compliance requirements, there may simply be no assumptions that cannot be challenged on how to get products to market. What many of these companies do is eschew the common refrain of, "This is how we have always done it". China collapses time by bringing fresh eyes to every industry – every step along the way is open for interrogation and improvement. Teams are challenged to ask themselves what can be parallel-pathed, what can be treated as a "launch and learn" approach, what can be radically simplified – or dropped altogether?

What this requires is a more careful and considered approach to risk management. For example, when work streams are parallel-pathed, there is a reasonable chance that they will not dovetail. Organizations must assess the cost-versus-benefit relationship of these types of enablers of time savings and be prepared with alternate plans should the original plan fail. One way to commercially assess this is to evaluate the opportunity lost by failing to have speed to market. For example, in the case of automotive this was quantified as US$2bn for a four-month delay. Thus, a plan with a risk of US$250,000 would be well justified. Or potentially, as in the case of Huawei, for whom the risk was falling back on a standard timeline if the chip and the handset workstreams did not merge, the risk was more an opportunity cost of resources that could have been used on other projects, should the parallel-pathing approach have not paid off.

But perhaps what is most compelling is that by challenging

sacred cows and learning along the way, even in the face of possible failure, organizations have the potential to shift their culture in the process – creating teams that collaborate as creative problem-solvers, individuals that challenge conventional ways of working, and stimulating businesses to take risks that lead to breakthroughs.

Seek Strategic Partners

Today, Nio has its own production sites, but when they launched their first vehicles, they were made by OEM partners. Why shouldn't an organization focus where it feels it can make the most difference and acquire strategic support from partners? This is fundamentally different from outsourcing – the key difference being the sharing of incentives and risks. Traditional outsourcing is about division of labour to complete tasks that are typically more cheaply or quickly done outside the organization, whereas strategic partnerships generally leverage depth of experience to go beyond what the organization is capable of currently delivering.

Sun Tzu says in The Art of War, "If you do not seek out allies and helpers, then you will be isolated and weak."[169] Yet, with any ally, whether in business or politics, the key to a successful relationship is alignment and incentives. Specifically, when managing strategic partners (versus simple outsourcing), the risks, costs and rewards of doing business together must be distributed fairly across the network. This starts with the alignment of objectives and outcomes, and the incentives to drive those – when the originator wins, the partner wins and when the originator loses, the partner loses.

When objectives are agreed, key metrics or key performance indicators (KPIs) measure the delivery of those objectives,

---

169. Sun Tzu, *The Art of War* (Filiquarian; First Thus edition, 2007).

generating accountability and enabling transparency across the partners, which can help avoid the traps that come from information asymmetries. While it seems obvious that partners would strive to agree on objectives when putting agreements together from the very beginning, it is often the case that these are glossed over in a hurry to get the deal done. This can be especially true for partners in the same industry who often assume that because they are from the same world, their motivations are also the same. These types of mistakes can be at best, costly, and at worst, prevent the partnership from achieving any success.

Communication and collaboration in these partnerships is critical, to avoid challenges such as excess inventory, or conversely lack of inventory, inaccurate forecasts or even poor sales efforts or customer service. Linked to this is the need for strong coordination to manage and control for risk when adverse events inevitably do arise.

Avoid Misaligned Incentives

Charlie Munger, Vice Chairman of Berkshire Hathaway, once said, "Show me the incentives and I will show you the outcome."[170] Let's apply this in a simplistic way in the case of personal finance to understand the principles more clearly. The average investor often bristles at the notion of paying someone a salary to manage their portfolio – this stems from the belief that they should pay for results. And so the industry that has arisen from this deep-seated consumer perspective is one of hidden fees, load fees, and commissions on trading and transaction fees. If you have a personal finance manager

170. Dr. Peter Munger, "Following the Money: Show Me the Incentives and I Will Show You the Outcome", Simon Kucher Consultancy blog article, July 31, 2018. https://www.simon-kucher.com/en-us/blog/following-money-show-me-incentive-and-ill-show-you-outcome

earning their commission on transaction fees, they are more likely to make more trades and buy and sell more. More transactions mean more fees that cut into the profits of any trades and further can result in triggering capital gains taxes – both of which can substantially wipe out meaningful returns. In other words, nothing about this incentive system is linked to the desired investor outcome of growing their wealth. This is a classic case of misaligned incentives in partnership and serves as a powerful reminder that we all need to be moving towards the same, clearly defined, goal – even more important when we are moving at pace towards the goal.

Expect Resistance to Change

As we have learned, society in China is hyper-responsive and adaptable based on the amount of change people have personally seen and experienced in their lifetimes. They are willing to consider new ways of doing things and openly embrace new products and technology. It is unlikely that this is the case in the Western world at such a broad societal level – perhaps amongst some younger generations, but not with society at large.

As such, with consumers, Western businesses will likely need to think about how to target the most receptive consumers and audiences, how to eliminate switching pains or costs, and how to ease transition for a broader base of users. Complementary approaches, partnerships or even infrastructure may be needed to help consumers time-travel to the future. It is not enough to simply "build it and they will come"; it is more about how to reward the transition to new behaviours and how to make adoption frictionless.

The same will be true within businesses with the employees and possibly even management. Classic examples of this are already seen in the West with the demise of industry stalwarts like Kodak cameras and film as well as with Blockbuster video rentals, who neglected to pivot, despite ample opportunities to capture the future potential that was laid at their feet. Yet the lesson is still not fully captured in the Western psyche – industries can and will be disrupted by unconventional thinking. Change is the only constant. With this in mind, visionary leaders must find ways to convince and inspire their own teams to time-travel and imagine new futures. Much as there is a need to incentivize behaviour in strategic part-nerships, there is the same need within the original business to drive a flexible, innovative culture.

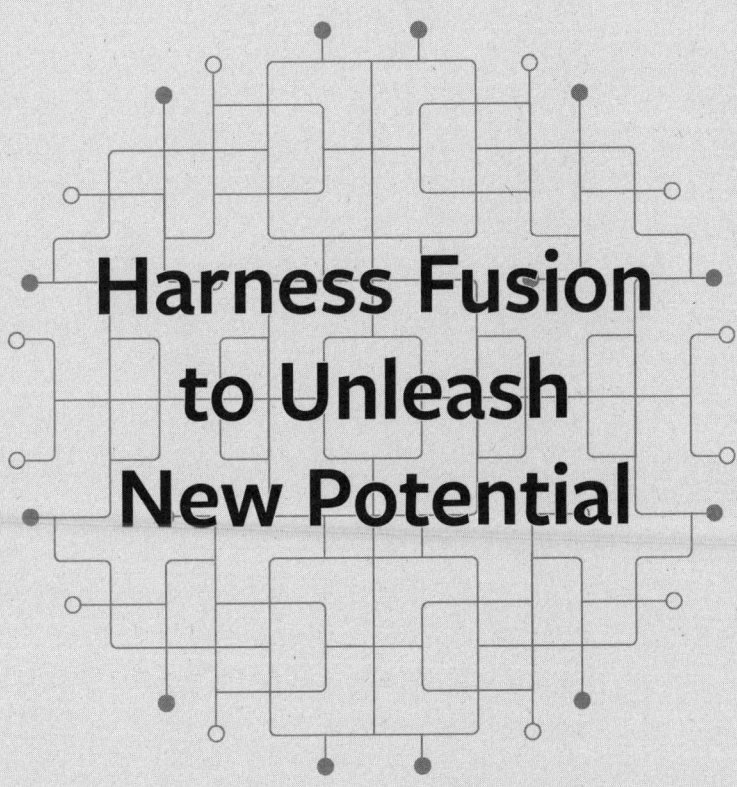

Chapter 11

Harness Fusion to Unleash New Potential

CATALYST 9

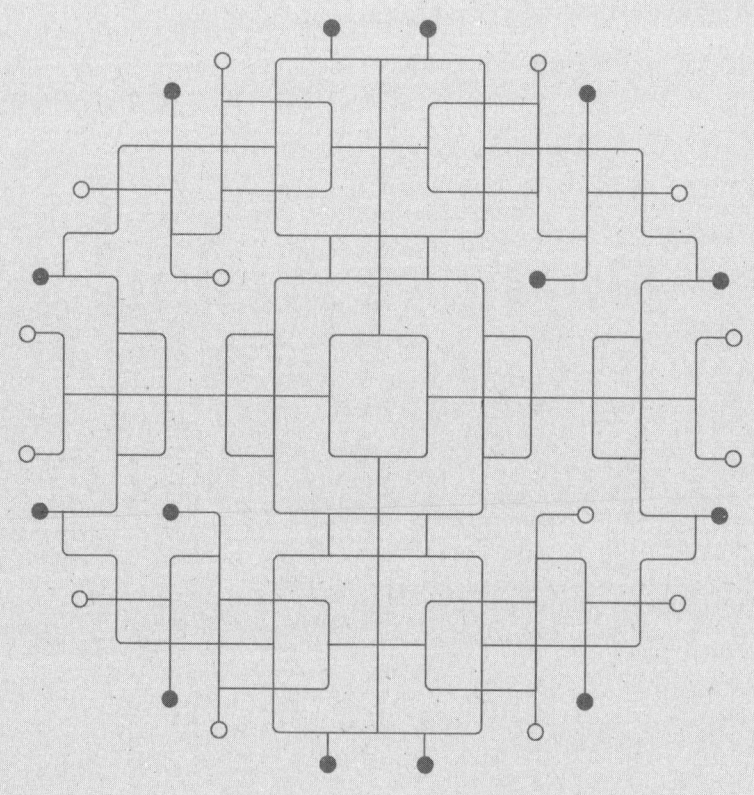

IN THE 1930s, Nobel Prize winner Hans Bethe discovered that when two hydrogen atoms collide, their nuclei fuse to form helium atoms, and in this nuclear fusion, new energy is released. When entrepreneurial and innovation fusion truly happens China-style, it indeed looks a lot like nuclear fusion. Business models are routinely mashed up, intertwined, and fused to release new business potential. There is no sense of "staying in your lane"; everything is game for combination. E-commerce companies fuse with banking to create microfinance (Alipay Group), social network businesses fuse with e-commerce to form social commerce (Douyin, Xiaohongshu), startup beverage companies fuse tech company business models onto soft drinks (Genki Forest), mobile phones fuse with IoT and even extend into electric-powered personal transport (Xiaomi), and quick-service fast food brands fuse internet and gaming technologies to transform their companies (Yum Brands China/KFC). In China, these fusions release an extraordinary new energy that disrupts entire industries and often even entire economies.

It might be easy to think of these fusions and multi-lane expansions as the result of a protected China business market which enables local brands limitless expansion to meet consumer needs due to the restraints around other international brands, and this wouldn't be entirely wrong. Consider Li-Ning, the Nike of China: Would Nike ever launch their own version of Starbucks in the US as Li-Ning has done with Ning Coffee in China? Likely, no. Would consumers accept it, and what would be the strategic rationale as F&B is a lower-margin business compared to apparel? Some of the choices of Chinese brands are admittedly puzzling. But what is most relevant for extrapolation and growth globally are the businesses that co-opt other businesses models outside of their own industry to disrupt and grow in China. Genki Forest, referenced in Chapter 9, harnessed data and technology to disrupt one of the few remaining traditional industries in China, soft drinks and beverages. Douyin, referenced in Chapter 4, fused social and commerce to explode online purchasing. These disruptions have in fact transformed industries both inside China and globally, which should leave business leaders outside of China questioning their hesitations around pivoting, shifting or fusing business models. In China, businesses like the country's leading gaming company Tencent are reimagining the future experience of personal transport for the coming generation of drivers and passengers who are heavily into gaming. By fusing their business with the EV market, they are mashing up two very different business models and economies to release new potential. Are companies in the US like Activision Blizzard or Electronic Arts or even Ford or General Motors thinking similarly? Why not?

Businesses and corporates in the West have a greater tendency to become myopically focused on their current categories, their existing competitors – and as a result, they become ripe for disruption by these Chinafied fusion business models. What Chinese businesses are doing, domestically and overseas, is bringing in business models and/or ways of working to disrupt traditional, slower-moving industries – and doing it successfully.

Yatsen: The Beauty Tech Game-Changer

After four years of eye-popping growth, Chinese beauty unicorn Yatsen Group made history as China's first beauty brand to go public, launching its offering on the New York Stock Exchange in November 2020. The company's multiple beauty brands – some of their own creation and others acquired – had become the #1 selling brands online in China's fast-growing e-commerce market. Founded in 2016, Yatsen Group is the creation of Proctor & Gamble (P&G) alum and Harvard Business School graduate, Jinfeng (David) Huang.

While at P&G in the market research department, Huang noticed that the market leaders were all foreign – L'Oréal, Estée Lauder, LVMH and P&G dominated the Chinese beauty market. Further, he observed they were all competing rather conventionally – using high-cost television advertising and high-profile celebrities to build brand awareness while focusing on physical retail and beauty advisors for product recommendations and ultimately make the sale. While this had been an effectively path to growth historically, he spotted a potential gap that he believed could not only be filled by a local Chinese brand but might also disrupt the entire industry in China. Seeing where China was headed in terms of digital and e-commerce and that younger Chinese consumers and beauty enthusiasts were starting to get heavily engaged in social media platforms like Xiaohongshu (RED), Huang saw an opportunity for a beauty company that behaved differently from the international players and was more tech-savvy, better reflected local consumer preferences and overall was more responsive to local consumer needs.

In fact, the rising generation of Millennial and Gen Z Chinese consumers were more likely to embrace local brands, which were untarnished by the quality scandals of previous generations. They felt proud to buy and use these brands. Not only that, consumers also had complaints about foreign beauty brands. Specifically in colour cosmetics, many Asian consumers struggled to navigate the colour palettes that were not designed for Asian skin tones, failing to provide the necessary colour range. In consumer research, many younger consumers reported finding international brands confusing and shared the sentiment that "Chinese brands know what is good for local consumers".[171]

With this backdrop in mind and fresh from school with an MBA from Harvard, Huang formed the Yatsen Group. Yatsen was named as such because it was the name of Huang's undergraduate university, Sun Yat Sen, which was in turn named after the first President of the Republic of China. Like Sun Yat Sen, Huang felt this company would also represent a new possibility for China – a Chinese-born beauty brand for Chinese consumers. Huang's ambition was to unseat the market leaders in colour cosmetics at the time – L'Oréal, LVMH and Estée Lauder held a combined 47.8%[172] market share – and to do so with a completely different approach to the market. Huang intended to combine his knowledge of the beauty business with his understanding of the digital ecosystems of China to create a business model that was a fusion of beauty and tech to disrupt the industry.

171. Sophie Yu and Scott Murdoch, "'All girls, buy it!' In China, Perfect Diary gives cosmetics world a makeover with live streams, low prices", Reuters, August 26, 202. https://www.reuters.com/article/us-china-cosmetics-perfectdiary/all-girls-buy-it-in-china-perfect-diary-gives-cosmetics-world-a-makeover-with-live-streams-low-prices-idUSKBN25M0BP
172. Shunyang Zhang and Sunil Gupta, "Perfect Diary" Case Study, Harvard Business School, August 20, 2021.

Yatsen Group's first move was to create three different colour cosmetic brands. With colour cosmetics being largely fashion- and trend-based, Huang felt there was too much risk in one brand alone and that a portfolio of brands would mitigate risk in case one or two of the brands were underperforming at any given time. The first brand created was Perfect Diary – a colour cosmetic brand targeting Millennials and Gen Z with a slogan of "Unlimited beauty". The slogan represented the value proposition: good quality at attractive prices, enabling consumers to buy many colours, play, and experiment. The business started online, primarily selling through Alibaba Group's Taobao and TMall channels and later launching sales platforms on social platforms including Xiaohongshu, TikTok/Douyin and WeChat through the Mini-Programs function. Perfect Diary was a major success, being the first domestic colour cosmetic brand on the infamous 11.11 shopping day to hit RMB100m (US$14.1m) in sales on TMall in 2018.[173] Within five years, largely based on the success of Perfect Diary and its position as the #1 domestic cosmetic brand in China, Yatsen Group conducted an IPO on the New York Stock Exchange (NYSE) with a valuation of US$4.46bn.[174]

So what specifically was the tech approach Yatsen Group took to disrupt the industry and build a unicorn beauty business in China? Unlike their foreign competitors with large R&D and marketing teams, the Perfect Diary staff is dominated by data scientists and

173. Daxue Consulting, "Perfect Diary Case Study: How this Chinese Makeup Brand Got to the Top", Daxue Consulting, March 7, 2021. https://daxueconsulting.com/perfect-diary-case-study-how-this-chinese-makeup-brand-got-to-the-top

174. Lawrence Nga, "Hillhouse backed Yatsen is Now Public. Here's What Investors Should Know", The Motley Fool, December 2, 2020. https://www.fool.com/investing/2020/12/02/hillhouse-backed-cosmetics-company-yatsen-ipo/

programmers. They have built an AI- and data-driven business which keeps getting smarter and smarter.

Perfect Diary leveraged China's Key Opinion Leaders (KOLs) with large followings on social media. In fact, there are over 3m KOLs in China, so many that there is a five-tier ranking system on the basis of how many followers each KOL maintains. The top tier KOLs have more than 5m followers, middle-tier KOLs in the region of 300,000–1m followers, and the lowest tier around 100,000 followers or fewer. Perfect Diary saw a role for all tiers and developed its internal team and database measuring the performance of each of their 15,000 KOLs.[175] The system measured various KPIs, including number of followers, number of active followers, post views, number of likes or favourites on posts, number of comments, number of forwards or shares, and more. The aggregate analysis resulted in a content engagement score which was used to evaluate each KOL's impact for the brand. This was then input into a model that linked these to brand sales. The outcome of this was more effective utilization of KOLs, resulting in stronger ROI for KOLs for Perfect Diary versus other competitors.

Perfect Diary managed the KOLs closely, providing content guidelines and co-creating content with them. For example, they chose four specific KOLs whose appearance and personality were well suited to Perfect Diary's four Animal Eyeshadow Palettes, with each representing a different palette that best suited them – resulting in more than 200,000 of the palettes being sold in a single week.[176]

---

175. Zhang and Gupta, "Perfect Diary" Case Study.
176. Zhang and Gupta, "Perfect Diary" Case Study.

Perfect Diary also used KOLs to develop new product innovations. Huang explained, "When we develop a new product, we send samples to 1,000 to 2,000 KOLs to try it. Maybe 50% to 60% of KOLs like it and are willing to promote it to their fans and tell them that Perfect Diary is planning to launch this new and exciting product. But at this time consumers cannot buy it – it is only available to KOLs. If we get positive response to KOLs' postings, we launch the product for consumers, and the early buyers are also excited to talk about the product on social media."[177]

Further, KOLs can propose new product ideas based on their insights of their followers. Certain shades were proposed by KOLs and they could even have customized packaging specially for their fans. Once such product, the Chinese Geography Eyeshadow Palette was ranked number three on TMall and was viewed over 180m times.[178]

Products were also co-created with KOLs. One such product was the Puppy Eyeshadow Palette which was developed with Li Jiaqi, the most famous beauty KOL and livestreaming salesperson. The shades in the palette were based on the colours of Li's own dog, thus the "puppy" name. Known as the "King of Lipstick", with 44m followers on TikTok/Douyin and 4m followers on TMall, Li pre-sold 150,000 palettes before launch, and 300,000 more were sold in seconds during the official launch livestream in March 2020.[179]

Perfect Diary also did unexpected collaborations with China's *National Geographic* magazine, China Aerospace, the British Museum, New York's Metropolitan Museum of Art and the

177. Zhang and Gupta, "Perfect Diary" Case Study.
178. Zhang and Gupta, "Perfect Diary" Case Study.
179. Daxue Consulting, "Perfect Diary Case Study".

Discovery Channel. All put forward uniquely themed palettes that became collectibles and increased consumers' esteem of the brand due to the cultural linkages.

This prolific innovation meant that Perfect Diary had an enormous number of SKUs – over 1,000 – much more than their competition. By contrast the L'Oréal portfolio had around 150 SKUs. This variety allowed Perfect Diary to satisfy very niche preferences of consumers in a way that other brands did not. Also, because the product was sourced from third-party suppliers, Perfect Diary could be quite nimble in getting products to market. Huang believed this was a key brand difference for Perfect Diary: "A large number of SKUs might not make sense for L'Oréal, but for us it is very meaningful because we use the AAARRR growth hacking framework (Awareness, Acquisition, Activation, Retention, Revenue, Referral). We worked with KOLs to satisfy the niche preferences of their fans with different SKUs as a pilot. Once it was proven to be a high potential product, we extended to reach and acquire more customers. Even if 1% of our 60m customers prefer a particular colour or shade, it is a market of 600,000 customers. Even 0.1% of customers translates to 60,000 customers and we can serve them economically. And once the consumer knows that Perfect Diary will take care of my everyday needs including my niche preferences, consumer engagement level is very high."[180] By early 2021, Perfect Diary had over 50m followers across its various platforms and enjoyed an unheard-of e-commerce repurchase rate of 40%.[181]

Perfect Diary also engaged with consumers post-purchase and ultimately brought them onto their own direct sales channel,

180. Zhang and Gupta, "Perfect Diary" Case Study.
181. Zhang and Gupta, "Perfect Diary" Case Study.

effectively converting public traffic (from other platforms) to private traffic (brand-controlled platforms). This is important as the costs of public traffic are steeply rising for brands in China, whereas the brand can better control the costs of private traffic, thus protecting their margins. How this worked for Perfect Diary is that across all e-commerce platforms, once a purchase was made, the consumer was invited to join a Perfect Diary WeChat group chat. These were chat rooms of up to 500 individuals with the chat hosted by a virtual AI-enabled beauty advisor who had a profile and appearance similar to the target consumer in order to make them feel more at ease and as if they were talking to a girlfriend. There were two types of chat groups depending on where the consumers had been sourced. One type of consumers were those who had purchased through an online e-commerce or social commerce platform and joined through a promotional lucky money card containing a discount on the next purchase. The other were consumers who had joined from offline pop-up stores or giveaways where they had scanned a QR code. The virtual beauty advisors communicated with consumers differently, using different tactics based on the source of recruitment and based on data-driven insights on how each group might be converted to purchase. Across both types of groups, AI beauty advisors shared tutorials on various products, answered any questions, and shared information on upcoming promotions and events. This had the impact of linking the consumers directly to the brand regardless of the original channel of purchase and meant that they could easily repurchase directly from the brand. It was observed that repurchase rates were even higher in these WeChat groups than on e-commerce.

Perfect Diary created a unique digital data platform, structured around the consumer with a single digital ID, which the Yatsen Group can use across all brands in the portfolio making it an extremely powerful platform for growth. There's no multi-brand competitor that can say the same, as most customer insights and information live under individual brands. For example, consumers might be on Shu Uemura's database but this does not ladder up to a broader L'Oréal database that is accessible by other brands in the portfolio. In fact, the virtual beauty advisors on WeChat have the option to link users to Perfect Diary or one of the other Yatsen Group brands, depending on what might best suit the user's needs. Thus, Perfect Diary and Yatsen can as easily be thought of as owning a consumer segment, which they happen to sell a portfolio of colour cosmetics to, but the group could easily extend into other segments of interest to their consumer base.

In fact, in 2020, Yatsen Group purchased French skin care brand Galénic, European luxury skincare brand Eve Lom and Chinese derma-skincare brand Dr. Wu to do just this. Huang explains, "A single brand may fall in and out of favour, but a portfolio can probably stay on trend for a long time. Different brands follow different paths and it's hard to get every single step right. But at least we can build the infrastructure that benefits all. By infrastructure, I mean our supply chain, marketing machine, distribution channels and product experience. It's like we built the road for Perfect Diary. Other brands can run on the same road, but we don't just focus on the road ahead. We envision a highway and build it. Since we built a highway, we want more cars on it. Either we start new brands, or we buy existing ones. The latter is faster. Most of our supply chain, marketing, and IT processes can be directly adapted to new companies."[182] It

182. Lou Qiqin, "Obsessed by Products: A Look Inside Huang Jinfeng's Perfect Diary", Interview with Jinfeng Huang, Jiemian Global, November 30, 2021. https://en.jiemian.com/article/6862046.html

has been estimated that with this Direct to Consumer (DTC) tech stack for e-commerce, marketing and consumer engagement, Yatsen Group could have any new brand – acquired or newly created – up and running and fully functional on e-commerce in a mere one to two days.[183]

To further drive the sales through the private traffic channel, in 2019 the Yatsen Group started to open retail stores. The business had an ambitious plan to open 600 stores in two years but rollout was slowed by the pandemic. As of June 2022, Perfect Diary operates approximately 200 stores in China. The role of physical retail is two-fold: the first is to provide an immersive brand experience for consumers to play and experiment with products; the second is to convert offline shoppers into online private traffic owned by the brand. The business estimates that 65% of the store shoppers are new to the brand and thus represent private traffic conversion opportunities.[184] After purchasing products in stores, shoppers are given free gifts as incentives to enter the Perfect Diary WeChat groups. This is a market strategy that has served as a guide to many other competing brands on how to regain control of their customers and convert them into private traffic.

In summary, Yatsen Group was created on the basis that two types of businesses could be fused – beauty and tech/social – and in the process create disruption and generate value. In leveraging behavioural, market, social and sales data, Perfect Diary has not only been able to stay ahead of trends better than competitors, but it has also been able to create and lead these trends. It has effectively

---

183. Tech Buzz China by Pandaily Podcast, Episode 84, interview with Gary Liu, CEO, South China Morning Post, January 14, 2021.

184. Daxue Consulting, "Perfect Diary Case Study".

changed product development from a more creative expression informed by R&D to a data-driven science with a pace and pulse that is more like a tech company. Perfect Diary takes products from concept to launch in less than six months, which is markedly faster than their global peers, which can take 9–18 months to get a new product to market. And the results of this approach are abundantly clear – in just three years, Perfect Diary has leapfrogged entrenched international rivals such as L'Oréal's Maybelline and Estée Lauder's MAC brands to become China's #1 colour cosmetic brand. With more than 50m followers on social media it can now reach and sell to its audience directly with near-zero marketing expense. This creates a growth flywheel which has higher sales conversion, at a fraction of the typical industry cost. This tech-enabled, data-driven beauty model has seen astounding growth of 327% from 2018 to 2019, outpacing the top 10 market players, growing customers by 49% to 23m at the time of its IPO in 2019.[185]

In 2020, Yatsen Group decided it was time to take its fusion beauty-tech business model abroad, launching Perfect Diary in Southeast Asia. Within a year the brand had coveted top sales spots in multiple markets. By May 2021, Perfect Diary was #1 in lip sales in Malaysia, #1 in colour cosmetics in Singapore and Vietnam, and #1 in loose powder in the Philippines.[186]

Also in China, despite the pandemic and contraction of planned retail store openings, sales were up 70.2% in the second half of 2020 in China (following lockdowns in Q1 and Q2); and as of end 2021, Yatsen Group was valued at US$12bn.[187]

---

185. Nga, "Hillhouse backed Yatsen is Now Public".
186. Julienna Law, "Can Perfect Diary Take C-Beauty Global?", Jing Daily, July 20, 2021. https://jingdaily.com/perfect-diary-c-beauty-global-expansion/
187. Ching Li Tor, "Perfect Diary's Parent Company Yatsen Lists on the US Stock

How to Export This Catalyst

What principles can be gleaned from Yatsen Group and Perfect Diary about the potential of fusion to Chinafy businesses, disrupt through business models and transform industries to explode potential anywhere in the world?

Look for the Goliaths and Disrupt like David

David and Goliath is a classic biblical tale in which a smaller, younger, unarmed and untrained David triumphs against a giant, well-armed, experienced warrior, Goliath. Fundamentally it is a story of courage and resilience, but also serves as a metaphor in business for how a smaller company lacking resources and experience can triumph against a well-established, deep-pocketed incumbent. In the tale, when David challenges Goliath, the giant laughs at the young shepherd boy's size and age. Then to everyone's surprise, David fells Goliath by throwing and lodging a simple river stone between his eyes.

Large, slower-moving industries – or Goliaths – are ripe for disruption with the application of tech/data-driven or other business models. In the case of Yatsen Group, beauty represented this opportunity, and established players, playing the traditional game of multiple, complex sales channels and a high-cost advertising-driven demand-generation model, were easily disrupted with a tech startup approach. In the case of Genki Forest, beverages were similarly disrupted using a data-driven model to unseat established players like

Market", Beauty Tech Japan, medium.com, February 2, 2021. https://medium.com/beautytech-jp/perfect-diarys-parent-company-yatsen-lists-on-the-us-stock-market-here-s-a-look-back-at-its-bc83957c35b1

The Coca Cola Company and Pepsi. It's a classic case of David and Goliath on the commercial battlefield, but in this case the weapon is to Chinafy with a fusion of business models.

Goliaths are often found in industries that are well-established with sprawling infrastructures and established players who often fall into the trappings of the system and the decades of investment made. For this reason, they are often unwilling to disrupt the system, falling prey to the fallacy of sunk cost – being irrationally focused on past investments and costs instead of future costs and benefits, and maintaining approaches that are no longer in the business's best interests. Like Goliath, these businesses often become over-confident, and this over-confidence renders them blind to the opportunities that exist. As a result, they often fail to respond to tectonic shifts in their industries, become less responsive to consumer needs and therefore less relevant, leaving themselves ripe for disruption by the Davids of the world.

Avoid Capital Intensive Fusions

Typically, when fusing two business models, one or both should be "cost light" and/or "capital light" – meaning there is not a need for heavy investment in advertising or infrastructure such as property, manufacturing plants or equipment. When we look at the potential for tech to disrupt various industries, one of the clearest observations is that tech generally lightens or removes the invested capital previously needed in the disrupted industry. And when businesses generate greater returns on invested capital versus the industry standard, they almost always create value.

For example, in the case of Yatsen Group, they brought a low-cost consumer acquisition model with the use of e-commerce and social versus the existing model in beauty of high-cost advertising and investment in point-of-sale beauty counters staffed with beauty advisors. Further, only third-party contract manufacturers were used rather than their own R&D laboratories or manufacturing plants. This not only made the cost of sales lower, but also dramatically reduced the cost of product development and production – de-risking the enterprise and enabling flexibility.

This principle of fusion, and particular the injection of tech into many industries, has reshaped how brands and businesses start to think about and value content, with consulting companies such as Accenture in China seeking to apply frameworks and value mapping to help businesses understand where and how value is generated and thus what capabilities need to be built to be competitive now and in the future.

Create a Growth (Hacking) Flywheel

Yatsen Group created a platform for sustained disruption across multiple brands using the concept from tech of a growth flywheel. The data-driven flywheel enables the brand to generate business efficiently, using less resources and energy over time, building momentum for growth. Also known as growth-hacking, flywheels are incredibly common in the tech industry but less understood and utilized outside of it.

A flywheel enables brands like Perfect Diary to behave and iterate like a tech company, beta-testing products with KOLs and consumers, leveraging the full power of digital channels, building demand and private traffic and doing so with a cost structure that is likely to decrease over time rather than increase due to the efficiencies generated from the e-commerce tech stack and business model. The system also gets smarter and better over time, enabling the business to not only stay ahead of trends, but to actually create them.

Designing a business around a flywheel enables different strategic inputs and decisions about the business. The amount of energy generated from a flywheel depends on three things – how fast you spin it, how much friction there is, and how big it is. The most successful business strategies will address all three aspects. Firstly, the speed of the flywheel increases when force is added to areas that can have the biggest impact. In the case of Perfect Diary, this was seen in both innovative products (sourced from KOLs and consumer inputs) as well as the KOL marketing engine. Both had the impact of making the KOLs more famous as it gave them the cachet of having an inside track to beauty trends; and by making the customers or KOLs more successful, Perfect Diary could become more successful.

Secondly, while applying force to the flywheel, there is also a need to eliminate friction so that the speed and momentum can build up unrestricted. For example, the friction could be around internal processes, lack of depth of understanding of consumer insights and sales, or even where customers are coming from or what the pain points on the customer journey are. In Perfect Diary's case, they did this by investing in a large data science team. At any given time, approximately 6–20% of Yatsen Group staff are employed in a data science role[188] – this is markedly higher than the industry average and seeks to reduce friction on the flywheel.

Thirdly, the more speed is increased, and friction reduced, the bigger the flywheel can become. This is when momentum is generated and the system itself becomes the force that spins the flywheel.

---

188. Tech Buzz China by Pandaily Podcast, Episode 79, "Perfect Diary (Yatsen Group): Cosmetics Ecommerce Superstar and China's L'Oreal for the Digital Age", December 16, 2020.

In the case of Yatsen Group, the Perfect Diary platform was the engine that could be leveraged by multiple brands in the group, thus making the commercial potential of flywheel expansion exponential in nature.

Know the Consumer Better than Anyone Else

One key element that we see in Chinese businesses is that almost all businesses that rise to the top do so by knowing their consumers more intimately than their competition. Ideally when fusing business models, one of the models will enable a deeper understanding of the consumer than already exists with the other business model. In the case of Perfect Diary, the fused business model of tech/data with beauty brought the business closer to the consumer – closer than even the market leaders. By understanding the consumers' needs and wants better, Perfect Diary was able to deliver a value proposition that was irresistibly attractive. And even beyond that, they were able to not only engage with them more deeply on social media but also to continually surprise and delight them with innovation. This generally results in greater consumer retention and repurchase – and as seen in the Perfect Diary case, the repurchase rate was an unprecedented 40%. Further, when you know your consumers better than anyone else, this has the effect of turning them into advocates for the business and brand, which results in a no-cost word-of-mouth conversion channel for sales.

Knowing your consumers better also becomes a scalable platform for entering other industries – likely adjacent industries – that serve the same consumers. For example, Yatsen Group started in colour cosmetics but has since successfully extended into skin care, using the Perfect Diary growth flywheel and e-commerce tech stack to introduce their beauty-obsessed consumers to new brands and offers. Considering their young, style-conscious female target audience, perhaps fragrance, accessories, shoes or fashion could be next?

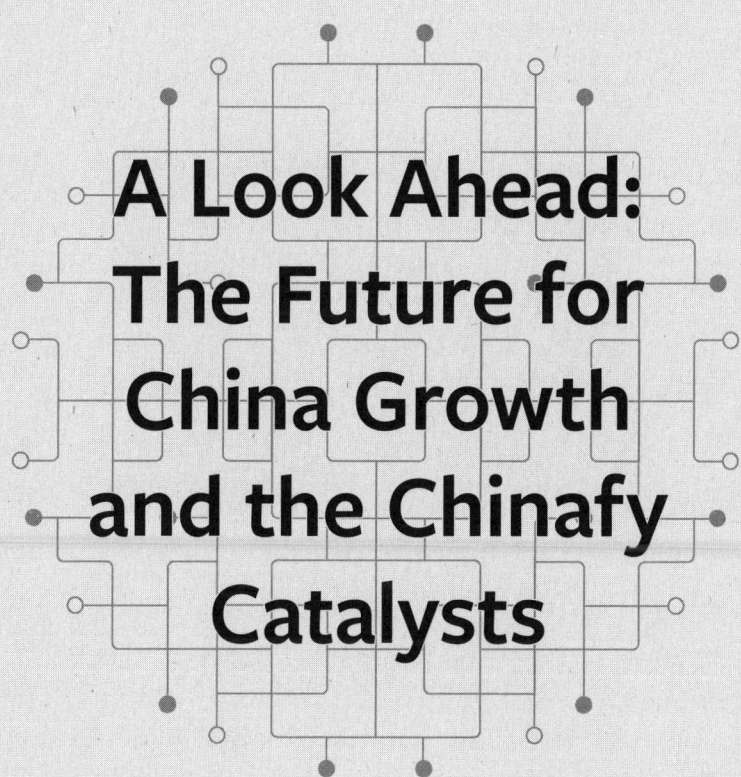

Chapter 12

A Look Ahead: The Future for China Growth and the Chinafy Catalysts

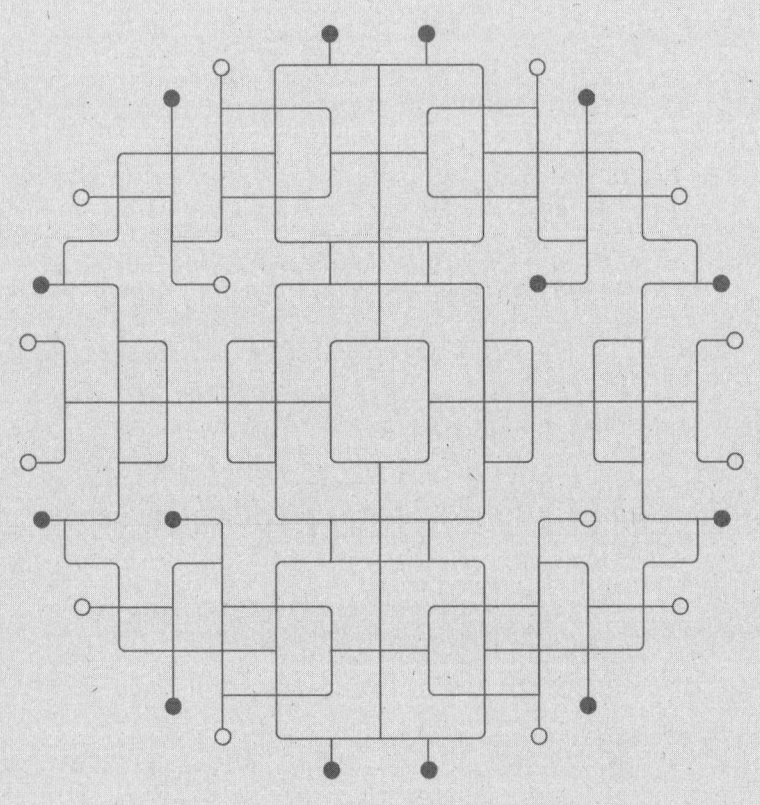

INNOVATION IS THE KEY that unlocks the potential for societies and economies to grow and thrive, evolving and progressing towards more promising futures. Those societies that push ahead in innovation will be the global thought leaders and superpowers of the world. Without understanding the very real success stories of Chinese innovation, it might be hard to imagine that the China of today is a nation well placed to be one of these superpowers. It might be yet harder still to imagine that we live in times where the innovation prowess and economic dominance of the West is no longer a given. However, the objective and undeniable reality is that China is a significant and driving force in the new economic reality of the world.

Luckily, success leaves clues. Businesses that succeed at the highest level are doing something different from others. The outstanding outcomes of Chinese businesses in China and globally are not a fluke. They are generally the product of a different approach, model, decision, or action that generates a different outcome. These "clues" are the Chinafy catalysts.

Yet, to truly embrace the Chinafy catalysts, we must overcome our Western bias when it comes to China and innovation. Ironically, increased exposure and exploitative interest in China have only served to bolster our beliefs in the West's dominance and our tendencies to discount China's growth, dismissing it as a "copycat" economy. Here is where we make a mistake – ignoring very real stories of innovation. Instead, we myopically focus on the social, ideological, and political differences we have with China. Global politics and the news media reinforce these views, highlighting the sensational negative stories of human rights and treatment of ethnic minorities and draconian zero-Covid controls that go viral and dominate the media landscape. This negative "evil" China narrative is sown so deeply that for the average person in the rest of the world, it overshadows the tremendous impact China is having in the global economy in business and innovation.

To have a comprehensive view and indeed be competitive in global business and innovation, we must be able to hold two truths in our hands simultaneously. China can be both ideologically different and in some cases in opposition to our Western beliefs and they can be out innovating the rest of the world and dramatically reshaping what it means to be globally competitive. *Chinafy* strips away, as much as is possible, the influence of government and politics on individual businesses to reveal what are some uniquely Chinese principles in innovation.

Indeed, the Chinese approach to accelerating and scaling innovation has enabled dazzling growth, new business models, disruptive digital ecosystems and value creation – delivering continuous economic growth in a way no other country has seen in all of history. This coupled with Europe's stagnated growth and America's economic, social, and political worries, leaves China poised to surpass the West in a matter of years, not decades. And with China's increasing impact in the global economy, the West is in danger of being not only disrupted but even worse, completely left behind.

Today, with pandemic-related border closures, the rest of the world views China from an even greater distance, and very decidedly from the outside looking in – unable to see the individual examples and stories of success. Further, as many Chinese businesses exist purely domestically or are unicorns in global industries that are less visible to senior Western business leaders personally (e.g., EVs, social commerce, fast fashion for teens), the eye-popping stories of global economic value creation do not materialize as sharply on our horizons. But by now, *Chinafy* has no doubt demonstrated that Chinese innovation is scaling at a pace that we need to understand.

The Chinafy catalysts, directly derived from actual companies disrupting the business landscape, bring forward the lessons and stories that savvy Western business leaders can leverage and emulate. Each catalyst is an independent learning and insight, yet if layered and combined in a modular fashion appropriate to the business challenge at hand, they can unlock exponential growth. And for application in individual businesses in the West, this is exactly what is recommended – businesses find the corollaries and inspiration from the catalysts and apply them one-by-one in structured and measured experiments to explore how any individual catalyst can stimulate the levers of business to drive rapid scale and accelerate growth.

In some of the cases and examples, there are also questions of social impact, ethics, and morality of innovation. For example, does the consumer or the world need more fast fashion like SHEIN as we attempt to reduce waste to deal with the pressing matter of climate change? What do we make of the Douyin/TikTok tech stack and the link to e-commerce and what it means for individual privacy or even responsible marketing and selling of goods and services to younger audiences? Do we really want EVs that are automotive shells for technology which become potentially disposable when technology rapidly advances? While some of the businesses in *Chinafy* do potentially present social and moral conundrums, the individual catalysts identified do have power and value beyond the industries they are applied to. As a caution, as we look to innovate and grow, we should also challenge ourselves to deliver innovations that not only have commercial value but also deliver this value with at minimum a neutral and ideally a positive social impact.

And even within these stories of innovation from China there are also examples we can look to for inspiration. For example, Pinduoduo, which links consumers directly to farmers successfully, delivers increased profits for farmers and decreased cost for consumers by cutting out the distribution middlemen, yielding a win-win for individuals on both sides of the transaction. Through reverse innovation, Xiaomi has put smartphones in the hands of some of the world's most economically challenged populations, transforming their lives with access to the internet.

So as we strive to innovate, we must be mindful of creating products and services that bring more value to the world, not just to the pockets of businesses. Thus, the innovation imperative is to create new possibilities with a sense of standards and responsibility – innovation can and should improve peoples' lives and the world around us. And when entrepreneurs and visionaries innovate with these aims in mind, the Chinafy catalysts can be used as levers to accelerate the spread of positive innovation.

China Aims for Global Innovation Domination

Chinafy represents a deep dive into existing business innovations with multiple years of results. It does not, however, dig into the longer-term, in-progress, government-driven advances happening in China in science, technology and invention. To understand where China's future lies in innovation, we must look beyond business to the world of emerging science and technology. This gives us a clearer picture of where China is headed, their ultimate aims and goals, and the sectors and industries they have ambitions to lead. While long-range science and technology investments are no guarantee of success, in practicality, we see that they generate a high probability for areas of future business innovation as scientific invention and innovation generally informs and trickles down to commercial application.

If we examine China as an international scientific contributor, in the early 2000s, there was a massive gap between the rest of the world and China's share of the top 10% most cited scientific publications, with China decidedly below the world average. However today, with a focus on the fields of chemistry, computer science, engineering, materials science, mathematics and physics, China has overtaken the EU and is close to the US in overall annual scientific research publication. China's annual gross domestic R&D investment has been substantially ramped up, reaching US$514.8bn in 2021, outstripping the EU at $390.5bn and nipping at the heels of the US at US$612.7bn.[189] Observers in the global scientific community expect the scale of investment to continue to grow as China's elite universities place increasingly higher in global rankings and as the educational system continues to annually produces more STEM PhD graduates than the US. In addition to increasing governmental spending and emphasis on education and R&D, China's private sector is also allocating increasing funds to the National Natural Science Foundation of China, which, like its Western corollaries, funds research-driven projects using rigorous, global peer-review standards. With this focus, in recent years China's science and technology

---

189. Carolina Wagner, et al., "What do China's Scientific Ambitions Mean for Science – and the World?" Issues.org, April 5, 2021. https://issues.org/what-do-chinas-scientific-ambitions-mean-for-science-and-the-world/

research workforce has grown rapidly to nearly 2m people.[190]

China is also soaring ahead in invention. "China has become a serious contender in the foundational technologies of the 21st century," stated a 2021 report from the Belfer Center at Harvard University.[191] In 2015, China also took the lead over the US in patent filings and continues to advance this lead. In 2021, China filed 68,720 patent applications, whereas the US filed 59,230, with the World Intellectual Property Organization (WIPO), the international system for countries to share recognition of patents.[192] The rate of increase from the previous year was higher for China at 16.1% versus 3% from the US, with the single largest filer for four consecutive years being China's Huawei Technologies Co. Ltd.[193]

Patents do not guarantee that an invention can be deployed or scaled for commercial impact. However, they are a reliable predictor of the probability of commercial impact as historically the number of patents filed is correlated with the overall rate of economic development. While we must also consider that there is the lag time between invention and commercial impact, what studies show is that with each successive decade, this lag time or gap is closing. What used to take more than 30 years from the year of invention to the year of commercial success (pre-WWII)[194] is now

190. Wagner, et al., "What do China's Scientific Ambitions Mean".
191. Economist Briefing, "China and the West are in a Race to Foster Innovation", *The Economist*, October 12, 2022. https://www.economist.com/briefing/2022/10/13/china-and-the-west-are-in-a-race-to-foster-innovation
192. Emma Farge, "China Extends Lead Over US in Global Patents, UN says", Reuters, March 2, 2021. https://www.reuters.com/article/us-un-patents/china-extends-lead-over-u-s-in-global-patents-filings-u-n-says-idUSKCN2AU0TM
193. Farge, "China Extends Lead Over US in Global Patents, UN says".
194. Rajshree Agarwal and Barry L. Bayus, "The Market Evolution and Sales Take-off of Product Innovations", *Management Science*, vol. 48, issue 8, 1024-1041, 2002.

often seen to be less than 10 years, depending on the sector.

China's acceleration in science, technology and invention is a plan that started 15 years ago when the government released its first National Medium and Long-Term Plan (MLP) for the Development of Science and Technology 2006–2020. The MLP launched the "Indigenous Innovation" (*zizhu chuangxin*) strategy and established goals, such as limiting imported innovation to 30%, to turn China into an innovation-oriented country, with a vision to become a world leader in science and technology by 2050.

This was seen as a grand experiment with questionable potential for success by the outside world. But when evaluating scientific publishing, government and private investment, the increase in STEM PhD graduates, researchers and patents, it can be observed that it has been a wildly successful plan thus far. This is why understanding and cooperating with China will be critical for the future of innovation globally. If managed collaboratively, vexing global issues could be jointly tackled, such as climate change and pollution as well as medical challenges such as pandemics and healthy life spans and could benefit the entire world across multiple dimensions – scientifically, socially, and economically.

In China, Change Is the Only Constant

China has been through rapid change since the time it began to open up and reform its economy in 1978. We must also acknowledge that China is going through another cycle of major change – in fact it seems that change is the only constant in China. Despite benefiting from 40 years of globalization and broad access to repositories of knowledge and information from Western education and businesses, Chinese leaders now question the degree to which globalization and the openness of the world economy is benefiting China, its culture, and its people.

Globalization brought Western ideologies to the youth of China, which started to shift social norms. This greatly disturbed Chinese leaders, who reacted by banning Western thought in Chinese schools and revisiting curriculums to increase the education on Chinese values and beliefs, making material like the book *Xi Jinping Thought* mandatory for high school students. While not overtly banning homosexuality, Beijing banned the use of effeminate men in popular media and TV, stating that "revolutionary culture" and "official morality" must prevail.[195]

Recent policies like the Dual Circulation Strategy aim to make China's economy less reliant on export and shift the balance more to China-for-China production. In the 5th Party Congress meeting in October 2021, Xi Jinping's speech highlighted his intent to make China wholly self-sufficient in food production as a matter of national security. In the same opening speech, he communicated his intent to continue to reform "unruly sectors" such as real estate, tech and after-school education. From business to education, there is a pronounced shift towards a more competitive, yet more controlled nationalist stance.

China has been actively working to close the loophole that allows Chinese firms to seek access to overseas capital markets via foreign IPO. It further blocks and penalizes those who attempt to go public even in domestic exchanges without the explicit blessing of the government. In 2020 when Alibaba's Ant Group, the financial

---

195. The Associated Press, "China Bans Effeminate Men from TV", npr.
        org, September 2, 2021. https://www.npr.org/2021/09/02/1033687586/
        china-ban-effeminate-men-tv-official-morality.

and lending side of the business, failed to get government regulators on side, China blocked what was anticipated to be the world's largest IPO in history at US$34bn[196] in a dual listing in both the Hong Kong and Shanghai stock markets. The IPO was anticipated to result in a valuation of $310bn, making Ant Group a peer of global banks like JP Morgan Chase.[197] The exact cause of the IPO cancellation is still not clear, but the regulators expressed that the application did not meet the requirements and following a face-to-face meeting with company heads including founder Jack Ma, the Ant Group quietly withdrew the listing and apologized to regulators for any inconvenience.

Another challenge to Chinese companies going public was witnessed with DiDi, the Uber of China. Within days of DiDi's listing on the NYSE, Beijing launched a cybersecurity probe citing data protection concerns for the ride hailing app. The app was removed from app stores and the system was prohibited from accepting new users during the investigation, which resulted in a loss of 85% of value from the US$14 IPO share price.[198] DiDi has since communicated it will seek to delist from the NYSE and plans to list domestically on Hong Kong's exchange.

Amidst the challenges in China with Chinese companies, there are also challenges by US regulatory agencies with Chinese-listed

196. Raymond Zhong, "In Halting Ant's I.P.O., China Sends a Warning to Business", *New York Times*, December 24, 2020. https://www.nytimes.com/2020/11/06/technology/china-ant-group-ipo.html

197. Raymond Zhong, "Ant Group Set to Raise $34B in World's Biggest I.P.O.", *New York Times*, November 6, 2020. https://www.nytimes.com/2020/10/26/technology/ant-group-ipo-valuation.html

198. Arjun Kharpal, "DiDi Shares Surge After Report that Regulators are Ending Probe", CNBC, June 22, 2022. https://www.cnbc.com/2022/06/06/didi-shares-surge-after-report-that-regulators-are-ending-probes.html

companies. In the US the NYSE began investigations on five China state-owned enterprises that were publicly listed, requesting documentation for compliance reasons. The Chinese government is refusing to provide this information for reasons of national security, thus forcing several companies to delist.

Experts and analysts see these curbs and brakes on Chinese companies trading publicly as part of China's bigger ambition to become a world technology superpower. But analysts differ on the government's motivations – some describing it as taking a moment to lay a solid regulatory foundation for public traded companies while others believe the motivation is about keeping domestic companies out of the hands of foreign investors. Either way, the outcome is the same, which is that the China tech giants are increasingly more closely guarded and brought on side to support Beijing's growth and development strategies. The Chinese government has even started to obtain "golden shares", which are ownership shares intended to provide direct oversight and control of companies with national interest in spaces like technology, the internet, and telecommunications. Golden shares give the government voting rights, and even veto power, allowing the government to steer and nudge private companies' strategies and development.

Meanwhile, the Western world is pondering the same – asking if deep connections with China remain prudent. Nations are expressing concerns about security as it related to using Chinese technologies in sensitive industries such as telecommunication and the internet. Countries have worries about the reliance on China manufacturing and production. And foreign governments even doubt the motivations of Chinese nationals who live and study or work overseas – are they simply on information-gathering expeditions? This might not be entirely unfair as the Chinese government does not consider these nationals "lost" but rather considers them "distributed resources".[199]

The most obvious manifestation in recent years of distrust and distancing was US President Donald Trump's trade war with China beginning in 2018 which aimed to equalize trade between the nations. However, to date, this effort is largely regarded as having been unsuccessful for the US. More recently in October 2022, the Biden administration advanced and strengthened this policy trajectory, clamping down on selling chip-making equipment and semiconductors to China. Earlier in July 2022, the US was blindsided when China released a semiconductor whose circuits were 10,000 times thinner than a human hair,[200] particularly concerning as chip manufacturing is believed to be a measure of national power. While it is unknown if China can scale this technology, as a measure to limit and control China's power, the US government effectively choked off access to the supplies China needs to further advance supercomputer and artificial intelligence capabilities.

Both the drives in China, as well as in the rest of the world, point to a decoupling strategy for both China and the world. While US-China relations are most often in the world news, China's relations with the UK, EU and Australia are also at the weakest points in history. This is all taking place against a sweeping backdrop of increasingly nationalist leanings across many nations and a growing distrust of globalism.

199. Wagner, et al., "What do China's Scientific Ambitions Mean".
200. Ana Swanson and Edward Wong, "With new Crackdown Biden Wages Global Campaign on Chinese Technology", *New York Times*, July 22, 2022. https://www.nytimes.com/2022/10/13/us/politics/biden-china-technology-semiconductors.html

Why We Must Still Watch and Learn from China

Despite the mounting social and cultural inward focus within China, there is very much an outward drive for increasing economic and political influence and dominance on the world stage. China is building power through innovation and technology for increased global influence. In fact, many might argue that today China is less reliant on the world than the world is on China – and that the world has more to lose if China pulls back.

Meanwhile, in keeping with the policies engineered to do so, China's dependence on other nations – economically, financially and technologically – is continuously and dramatically declining. Further, in recent years with pandemic border closures and travel restrictions, China itself has become increasingly opaque to the outside world. Due to Covid restrictions, business travellers and foreign workers have rarely been granted entry permits to China and most Chinese nationals were not able to renew passports or apply for visas for travel to leave China. Even foreign press presence in China has dwindled. Some major nations like Australia, following escalating China-Australia tensions, now have no journalists present in the country. In its annual report published January 2022, the Foreign Correspondents Club of China, "denounced the regime's increasingly systematic weaponisation of foreign journalists' visas" – suggesting that China was using the system as a tool for diplomatic policy.[201]

---

201. Reporters Without Borders, "Foreign Correspondents' Presence in China Threatened by Visa Weaponization", January 22, 2022. https://rsf.org/en/foreign-correspondents-presence-china-threatened-visa-weaponisation

With this lack of visibility as well as China's rampant domestic censorship, there is an increasing gap in understanding on what is happening inside China with regard to business, the economy and society. The world often is forced to rely on any information that Beijing chooses to release, with some skeptics suggesting the official information likely represents an overly positive view. That is if information is even available. In October 2022, Beijing declined, without explanation, to release eagerly anticipated economic data which would have shed some light on the impact of the large-scale, rolling lockdowns as part of China's zero-Covid policy[202] – prompting concerns about not only the data itself, but also about the world's ability to rely on data availability in the future. But even the information the government does choose to release does not sound encouraging for China's economic growth.

For the first time in 30 years, China's GDP lags versus the entire Asia Pacific region.[203] At the time of writing in Q4 2022, the 2022 YTD GDP in China was estimated to be 3.2% for the year with 3% being attributed to the manufacture of Covid testing supplies.[204] Meanwhile, China's youth unemployment (those aged under 30) has reached an astounding 20%,[205] a record high for the nation. In

202. Thomas Hale, Hayden Lockett, et al. "China Delays GDO Data Release in the Middle of Communist Party Congress", *Financial Times*, October 17, 2022. https://www.ft.com/content/7fde9d30-0754-48cd-8502-658c175cd99b

203. Helen Davidson, "China Growth Lags Asia Pacific for the First Time in Decades as World Bank Cuts Outlook", *Guardian*, September 27, 2022. https://www.theguardian.com/business/2022/sep/27/china-growth-lags-asia-pacific-for-first-time-in-decades-as-world-bank-cuts-outlook

204. Kevin Yao, "China's Q3 Growth Seen Bouncing 3.4% but 2022 Set for Worst Performance in Decades", Reuters, October 14, 2022. https://www.reuters.com/markets/asia/china-q3-growth-seen-bouncing-34-2022-set-worst-performance-decades-2022-10-14/

205. Bloomberg News Desk, "China's Youth Jobless Rate Hits

Xi Jinping's speech at the 20th CCP National Congress in October 2022, there was a clear willingness to sacrifice short- and medium-term economic growth for a Covid victory, leaving the world to wonder if China's appetite for growth and its contribution to the world economy will regain its former momentum.

While some do wonder if China's glory days are over, we know China can mobilize and move fast when it wants to. So while enthusiasm may be dampening on China as an exploding economy with seemingly unlimited growth potential, only time will tell. What is increasingly relevant for consideration is that the slowing of the China market, as well as the ever more constraining government involvement on Chinese businesses, provides even more impetus for these brands to look overseas for growth and perhaps even for Chinese entrepreneurs to start businesses (like SHEIN in Chapter 9) that do not even compete within China.

Indeed, Chinese entrepreneurship is a fundamental part of the culture, which is why it is unlikely that the spirit and seeds of Chinese entrepreneurship will diminish. Chinese companies are already taking these breakthrough business models overseas and in fact there is a word for this in Chinese: *chuhai*. Chuhai literally means going overseas to look for growth. We see this in markets where Chinese entrepreneurs spot an opportunity to export business models leveraging mobile internet. In India mobile internet is nascent, but fast growing, which presents an incredible opportunity to plug-and-play in the space of apps. In fact, today in India, 44 of the top apps (Google Play) are made by Chinese companies.[206]

Record 20% in July on COVID Woes", Bloomberg, August 15, 2022. https://www.bloomberg.com/news/articles/2022-08-15/china-youth-jobless-rate-hits-record-20-in-july-on-covid-woes#xj4y7vzkg

206. The Next Billion podcast, "Chu Hai: Why Chinese Entrepreneurs are

As Chinese businesses and brands aggressively explore global expansion, this means brands in the West will also face Chinese competitors head-to-head in their home markets. When confronting Chinese businesses on the industry battlefield, incumbents should expect to see these businesses use plays from the Chinafy catalysts to disrupt and shift the forces of competition. Understanding how to Chinafy and win will become essential not only for business on the global stage, but also may become relevant for local businesses unexpectedly facing global Chinese competitors for the first time.

With China's growing prowess in science and technology, it is unlikely that the long-term prospects of China are at risk. However, one might question the merit of looking to businesses in a struggling economy and the value of the Chinafy catalysts and learnings under the current economic trajectory in China. The recent situation with rigid zero-Covid policies, the trade wars with the US, and mounting tension with even Asian neighbours is undoubtedly concerning for China. No less concerning is the current recession and inflation in EU and US. And yet we still look to outstanding businesses who are innovating in these markets for inspiration. The current challenges in China and economic slowdowns do not negate the learnings from the last 20 years, a critical period in China's development. This is why the Chinafy catalysts that enabled this growth should be studied as the single most important innovation renaissance in modern times.

Why do we still study ancient Rome even though the Roman empire is a fallen empire? Ancient Rome has provided a goldmine of

---

Targeting Emerging Markets Across the World", GGV Capital, Season 1, Episode 28, 14 April, 2020. https://nextbn.ggvc.com/podcast/s1-ep-28-chuhai-why-chinese-entrepreneurs-are-targeting-emerging-markets-across-the-world/

ideas and concepts that are still in use in the modern world. Systems of laws and government, philosophy, architecture, language, and literature still inform us today. What set the Romans apart was their ability to take something and make it even better than before – in other words they were continuously innovating.

In summary, China's progress and ambition serve as a bold invitation to the West to open their eyes and reclaim their innovative roots. With China's well-prepared plan to become a technological superpower dominating the development of the 21st century, we can reasonably expect that China will be a leading force in the Fourth Industrial Revolution. It is highly likely, especially considering the current progress, that China could drive the future of robotics, the Internet of Things, virtual reality, and artificial intelligence. This, along with the fact that China currently represents one-third of the global economy, suggests that the rest of the world breaking ties and decoupling from China might ultimately leave international companies a few steps behind Chinese companies. To remain competitive, businesses need to study and, ideally, be where innovation is happening. And if China is driving the technological revolution, then global businesses with China operations will be present and able to export these learnings from China to their head offices. In other words, maybe it's time we start to copy China.